THE LAST JEW FROM WEGROW

The Memoirs of a Survivor of the Step-by-Step Genocide in Poland

SHRAGA FEIVEL BIELAWSKI

Edited and Rewritten by Louis W. Liebovich

PRAEGER

New York
Westport, Connecticut
London

Library of Congress Cataloging-in-Publication Data

Bielawski, Shraga Feivel, 1916–
    The last Jew from Wegrow : the memoirs of a survivor of the step-by-step genocide in Poland / Shraga Feivel Bielawski ; edited and rewritten by Louis W. Liebovich.
        p.   cm.
    ISBN 0–275–93896–4 (alk. paper)
    1. Jews—Poland—Wegrów—Persecutions. 2. Holocaust, Jewish (1939–1945)—Poland—Wegrów—Personal narratives. 3. Bielawski, Shraga Feivel, 1916– . 4. Wegrów (Poland)—Ethnic relations.
I. Liebovich, Louis. II. Title.
DS135.P62W613   1991
940.53'18'094384—dc20   90–24127

British Library Cataloguing in Publication Data is available.

Library of Congress Catalog Card Number: 90–24127
ISBN: 0–275–93896–4

First published in 1991

Praeger Publishers, One Madison Avenue, New York NY 10010
An imprint of Greenwood Publishing Group, Inc.

Printed in the United States of America

The paper used in this book complies with the
Permanent Paper Standard issued by the National
Information Standards Organization (Z39.48–1984).

10 9 8 7 6 5 4 3 2 1

The Last Jew
from Wegrow

This book is dedicated to the memories of
my wife, Esther,
my mother, Sarah Frieda Bielawski,
my first love, Rachel Mandelbaum,
all the Jews of Wegrow who died so tragically,
and the 6 million Jews who died at the hands of the Nazis.

Contents

Preface

My name is Shraga Feivel Bielawski, and I am a retired businessman who resides in Illinois. I was born in Poland in 1916, and I have three sons, all physicians, who live in the Midwest.

This book describes my experiences as a Jew in Poland. Mostly, I recall the miserable six years after the German invasion on September 1, 1939. Today, Germany has re-united, and Poland has a new, noncommunist leadership. The world is changing, but I know that, in some ways, the world remains the same. I see anti-Semitism wherever I go. In my home-town of Wegrow, Poland, I watched this anti-Semitism turn a tranquil life into a monstrous nightmare.

Some scholars claim that the Holocaust never occurred. Such asser-tions constitute a propaganda campaign against Israel and the Jewish people. In my worst dreams I could not have imagined that "historians" and "scholars" would attempt to deny the very existence of death camps and gas chambers, and that many thousands of their readers would be misled into questioning the sufferings and horrors of an entire generation.

Others say the Holocaust was not as bad as Jews claim. Many have forgotten about it. The rise of a new generation that has had only fleeting glimpses of the past makes the testimonies of Holocaust survivors sig-nificant. I pray that all who read this will learn what ignorance and prejudice can do to the human soul and to the human spirit. Could

neighbor turn on neighbor? Could good, hard-working, industrious people be machine-gunned to death and sent to gas chambers because they
prayed to their God in a different way?

Never again, I hope. To the doubters and to those who do not know
what happened, I say, "Read this book and never forget. It happened.
I was there."

*   *   *

A special note of appreciation is extended to my sons, Simcha Israel,
Yehuda Zev, and Mayer Abraham, for their hours of review and revision
of this book.

The Last Jew
from Wegrow

Chapter 1

Growing Up Jewish in Poland

I

The rural Poland of my youth, in the 1930s, was a beautiful land of
golden wheat fields, stately forests, peaceful villages, and rolling mead-
ows lined with gentle, unspoiled streams. People lived modestly in their
village homes or in well-kept farmhouses adjacent to picturesque barns
and sheds, typical of Poland because only 30 percent of the population
lived in cities and towns. Buildings that were hundreds of years old were
to be found even in small villages.

For centuries until the 1940s, Jews had played a strong and colorful
part in Poland's long, proud history and tradition. During the Middle
Ages, Jews had fled western Europe because of organized persecutions,
including the Spanish Inquisition, and the Polish nobility had welcomed
the Jews beginning in the twelfth and thirteenth centuries. Most of the
Jews who came to Poland were traders and businessmen. They provided
a spark to Polish commerce that the wealthy landowners desperately
needed. By the nineteenth century, over 80 percent of the world's Jews
lived in Poland. Most of the Christian Poles traced their ancestry to the
Polanes, a Slavic tribe that had settled in Poland in the tenth century.
German ethnics, who lived in areas near the western border, comprised
about 30 percent of the population. Family lineage of Jews and gentiles
could be traced back not years or decades but centuries.

Wegrow, a sleepy village of 11,000 persons, stood alongside the Liwiec River, just fifty-five miles northeast of the bustling capital city of Warsaw where the Vistula and Bug rivers converge. In the 1930s about 60 percent of the residents of Wegrow were Jewish and about 40 percent Roman Catholic, a large percentage of Jews even for Poland, where Jews comprised about 10 percent of the nation's 35 million people. Wegrow was in a farming area, where the Jews' skills as agricultural traders were needed, and over the centuries the number of Jewish people in the town had steadily increased. Many earned a living by creating Jewish religious artifacts such as prayer shawls and by copying Jewish scriptures. In business Jews dealt primarily with other Jews. As the main industry of the region became decreasingly important to their livelihood, the reason why Jews had originally come to the area became less obvious.

In those days, the fifty-five miles to Warsaw was a day's travel by horse and wagon. Warsaw was close enough to visit on business or for shopping, sightseeing, or browsing, but far enough away that it seemed to be part of another world.

The village was more than 700 years old. Nearly all the retail businesses centered around the busy town square, where buildings were as ancient as the village. The town's core stretched for about a mile. At one end of the square stood a great Roman Catholic Church with a huge spire that reached seventy feet above the ground and with two belltowers each containing an immense church bell that called parishioners to church on Sunday. Among the many businesses that edged the square were a pharmacy, a grocery store, my family's clothing store, a restaurant that both served food and sold packaged liquor, a state liquor store, and a store that sold caps. All the stores around the town square, except for three, were owned and operated by Jews.

A U-shaped parking and shopping area filled most of the center of the square. This central shopping area actually consisted of two old, brick buildings honeycombed with about a hundred tiny rooms each. In the rooms, townspeople sold everything from socks and bed linens to shoes and spices. Women often rented space so they could earn extra family money from their sewing or baking. Farmers came to town on Tuesdays and Fridays in horse-drawn wagons, parked the wagons in the square, unhitched the horses, and turned the animals to face the backs of the wagons so that the horses could feed while they rested and the farmers sold their products off the wagons. On these days, the square became a beehive of personal commerce as marketers and farmers haggled over the purchase and sale of fresh fruits, vegetables, eggs, butter, milk, cheese, and other farm products. Sometimes, there were as many as 500 farmers in the square. The rural visitors used their proceeds to buy whatever they needed for their homes and dinner tables. The square was transformed into a cacophony of squawking geese, cackling hens, bartering merchants and farmers, and people just socializing generally. During the winter, the snow was swept away from the square and the outdoor merchants set up umbrellas over their stalls in case more snow fell. I could watch all this activity from the front door of our store.

Townspeople did not need automobiles, because residents could easily walk across the city. Even in the late 1930s there were only two autos in the entire community and maybe two telephones. A commodities broker owned one phone, because he needed quick communication with Warsaw or other areas. The autos were owned by a wealthy physician and by a Polish aristocrat who lived on a baronial estate about twenty miles outside town. Buses frequently traveled back and forth from Warsaw. Those were the only mechanized vehicles we saw regularly.

Residential neighborhoods stretched in all directions from the center of town. The distance from one side of town to the other was about six miles. Small, five-to-six-room frame houses, with shingled or corrugated roofs, sat next to each other in rows along the rough, stone streets. Giant trees shaded the cement sidewalks, and flowers decorated lawns and stoops or entryways to the houses. By law, residents maintained clean, well-manicured front yards free of debris. Anyone who neglected a yard could be fined by the town council. The council was democratically elected, and a few Jews even served as aldermen. My uncle was a council member at one time. Backyards were small and not so neatly kept, because often small businesses, such as private leather-tanning operations, were operated in them. Wegrow's main manufactured product was leather. The town had many large tanning operations as well as small private ones.

Electric power had eased my parents' lives somewhat. A power plant, owned by a wealthy Jew, opened outside town just after World War I. Another Jewish man owned the town's sawmill. In fact, 75 percent of the businesses were owned by Jews.

In the late 1920s we were the first family in town to buy a radio, an oblong electric box about eight inches high and eighteen inches long. A radio station in town was owned and operated by the government, as were all radio stations in Poland.

Our building had no indoor plumbing. A well in the backyard provided water. We would drop a bucket into the water, fill it, and raise it to the top by cranking a handle at the side of the well. The bucket rose as the crank turned the windlass and the rope wrapped around a long slender pole across the top of the well. For baths, we would fill a wooden tub in the kitchen with water heated on the stove. We had electricity but few modern conveniences. For instances, we had no refrigerator or even an icebox. We stored food in the cellar to keep it from spoiling, but had to purchase staples daily, and that was why the market in the square was always crowded with shoppers. My mother and sister scrubbed clothes clean on a wooden washboard. A heating stove fueled by wood or coal stood between the living room and the kitchen and kept the house warm in cold weather. The five-room living area was located at the back of our clothing store, and our 30-by-350-foot lumberyard, filled with neatly stacked, freshly cut wood, sat behind the house.

An intricately carved set of wooden doors folded outward from the front entrance of our store. The doors formed a solid wooden facade across the front of the building when we pulled them closed and locked the store. Slender, vertical windows allowed a small amount of sunlight to peep into the clothing store during the day, and a second, narrow inside door with a brass handle could be pushed inward to gain entry to the store during business hours.

There were many newspapers in town, which could be purchased from street vendors. Five of them were Yiddish-language papers directed to the Jewish community, and one of these was a Zionist newspaper that devoted itself to the establishment of a state of Israel. The Christian-owned newspapers carried daily news, and often the reporting was couched in not-so-subtle anti-Semitic language. From time to time, Jewish residents would complain to the wealthy Christian newspaper publishers about the anti-Jewish tone, but to no avail.

Wegrow had two moving-picture theaters, and about once a month I would take a girlfriend to see an American film. My main source of knowledge of life in the United States came through these films with Polish subtitles. Shirley Temple was our favorite actress. I still can see her singing "On the Good Ship Lollypop." Christians and Jews sat together, and often we would chat outside the theater after the movie had ended. The movie theater was one area of common ground for both Jew and gentile.

II

I was born into a religious Polish Jewish family with a longstanding tradition. My father was Meir Wolf Bielawski and my mother was Sarah Frieda. They named me Shraga Feivel, after my father's great-great-grandfather, Shraga Feivel Danziger, the founder of the Aleksandrow dynasty of rabbis. A proponent of the Hasidic movement, he followed the teachings of the famous Baal Shem Tov, or "Master of the Good Name." Born Israel ben Eliezer, the Baal Shem Tov lived in Podolia, Russia, between 1700 and 1760. He was said to have performed miraculous cures by use of God's name. Early Hasidim were Jewish mystics who claimed knowledge of the word of the Lord and who eventually formed an Orthodox sect of Judaism. They adhered strictly to the words of the Torah (the five books of Moses), emphasizing fervent prayer and reverence of the rabbi as a mediator between God and the world.

For decades, the men in my father's family were Polish rabbis from Aleksandrow, but my father moved to Wegrow near the end of the nineteenth century to marry a Wegrow woman. She bore two children but died during the birth of her second child, and so, in about 1904, my father remarried. My mother, my father's second wife was then seventeen and he was thirty-four.

Religion played an important role in all those generations, down to my own. My father, who had attended *yeshivas* (Jewish centers of learning), in Poland, was learned in Talmud, (written commentaries on Jewish law). He spoke Polish and Yiddish fluently, which was necessary for dealing with both the Christian and Jewish populations. Yiddish, a combination of Hebrew and German, was used as a common language among European Jewry throughout the Middle Ages and into the twentieth century. Everyone in my family spoke Polish, Yiddish, and Hebrew, and most of us could speak some German and Russian. My father was an astute businessman. He had always said he never wanted to become a pulpit rabbi because he did not want to profit from teaching Torah, so he owned and operated both the clothing store and the lumberyard. He was scrupulously honest and extended credit to many Christian customers, primarily Roman Catholic farmers. He charged no interest and was well liked by everyone. The lumberyard brought in about $100 a week, from which we paid for part-time help, our taxes, and our raw materials. Of course, $100 in those days would purchase $1,000 worth of goods in 1990s dollars.

My mother actually oversaw the clothing store along with my sister, Menucha, who was three years older than I. My mother had little formal education but was a sharp businesswoman and probably a better salesperson than my father. The clothing store netted less money than the lumber business, but every little bit helped. My mother also had inherited from her father two small apartment buildings that she rented for extra family money.

My brother, Yitzchak, was ten years older than I, and my other brothers, Yerachmiel and Moshe, were three and five years younger. I began attending Hebrew school at age four, sitting through classes for six hours a day, six days a week. Two years later, I started classes at the local public school, attending from morning until early afternoon. In mid-afternoon I would walk to the rabbi's house, a few blocks away, to study Hebrew and religion until about nine o'clock.

My father was an imposing man with a stern, scholarly appearance. He wore formal clothes and a yarmulke (skull cap) all the time. He was partially bald with rumpled facial features and a large, hawk nose. Tufts of gray hair peeped out from under the skull cap and tumbled into sideburns. He had dark, piercing eyes that seemed to see all and know all. But his appearance belied his extraordinary personality. He had a marvelous sense of humor, and I used to laugh at his riddles and jokes all the time. After school he would occasionally sit in front of the clothing store and greet the children as they came by. "What is your name?" he would ask one of the little girls. "Rachel," she would answer. "Rachel," he would repeat, a sly smile spreading across his face. "That's a boy's name!" The little girl would look perplexed and say, "No, it isn't." "Yes, it is," he would respond and then burst into laughter letting her know it was all a joke.

My mother was more serious and wore modest, dark clothing, often with a shawl on her shoulders and a net covering her hair. She looked older than her years, especially after my father died. She had a wrinkled face with a large nose, but it was a kindly face that reflected her extraordinary powers of motherhood.

We were a close family, and the most pleasant memories of my formative years are of evenings when we used to play together in the yard. We would kick a ball around, wrestle, play tag, or engage in the other hundreds of activities that occupy children who have no television or radio. Our favorite game was war. We would choose sides and grab long sticks. Then each side would "shoot" at the other with the sticks, mowing down the enemy until the battle was over and the soldiers miraculously came back to life.

My father used to read us Bible stories and quiz us about how much we remembered and about the meanings of the stories. The Talmud meant everything to us, and my father knew every verse and every page without having to refer to the actual writings.

During the warm months we often packed a picnic dinner and found a deserted spot in a wooded area along a stream where we enjoyed an afternoon. The children would splash in the shallow water or tumble in the grass and then gather on the picnic blanket to enjoy the meal my mother had packed. Sometimes, friends would accompany us on our family picnics, always Jewish friends. At night, relatives or friends would come to our house and enjoy conversation and refreshments. Few of the visitors were gentiles. There was always that feeling of separation. When I reached my teens, I would walk through town and chat with others my age, some of whom were Jewish and some of whom were not. Although I had both Jewish and Christian friends, none of my close friends were Christian. As I grew older, the non-Jewish acquaintances grew more distant as they listened to their friends and parents speak ill of the Jewish people. We mixed with the gentiles, but we didn't.

The Jews were primarily retailers, merchants, and salesmen, trading in grain, cattle, and horses. Many worked in small factories and leather and parchment works, serving as scribes for the writing of Torah scrolls, *mezuzas* (wooden or metal cases enclosing small parchments containing passages from the Torah and attached to doorways), and *tefillin* (leather-encased scriptures worn on the forehead and left arm by Jews during morning prayers). Others were shoemakers, tailors, furniture makers, bricklayers, glaziers, and hat makers. Wegrow had its own Jewish doctors, dentists, lawyers, and writers. It had a Jewish bank, a home for the poor, and a hostel for strangers.

My favorite time of the week was the Sabbath, *Shabos*. The Jewish Sabbath begins at sundown on Friday and ends at sundown on Saturday. The Jewish tradition pre-dates the carefully kept time of the modern era, which is broken down into minutes and hours. Periods of sunlight and darkness marked time historically, not the noon-hour and the stroke of midnight. Jews have always maintained the tradition that each day begins and ends at sundown and so the Sabbath begins at sundown on Friday and ends at sundown on Saturday. Sabbath services are held at the synagogue on Friday nights and Saturday mornings. We all went to the synagogue before dinner on Friday and participated in the traditional Sabbath prayers. There was a Great Synagogue in Wegrow that was 200 years old and about ten smaller synagogues. Not all Jews were religious in the town. In fact, some rarely went to services, but the synagogue elders checked the square every Friday in the late afternoon to make certain that the businesses owned by Jews closed early. Jewish businessmen who violated the Sabbath could be severely punished by economic boycotts and by ostracism.

Always at the synagogue on Friday nights was a gathering of indigent Jews who were passing through town. They knew that if they came to worship on Friday night, someone from the town would invite them home to share a meal. Hospitality was an accepted practice. Any Jew passing through on any day could find lodging at a special hostel designed for just such wanderers.

When we returned home for the Sabbath meal with our dinner guests, we found a home given over to the Sabbath. The aroma of fresh-baked festive Jewish bread, challah, filled the house. The long, slender Sabbath candles sat on the dining room table in silver candlesticks waiting for my mother to utter the Sabbath prayer and kindle the lights that would once again illuminate the day of rest. A fine, clean, white linen cloth covered the table. After prayers we dined on gefilte fish, meat, vegetables, potatoes, and an assortment of desserts. Of course, we drank the traditional Sabbath wine to usher in the "Sabbath bride," as we called the holiday. My father sat at the head of the table, and it was understood that children did not talk during the meal.

Roughly half the students in the public schools in Wegrow were Jewish and half were Christian, and we all sat together in classrooms. We studied science, mathematics, Polish history, Polish literature, geography, economics—all the traditional academic subjects. Most of the teachers were Christian, but some were Jewish. Scuffles between the Jewish and Christian children broke out several times a month. Sometimes fights marred the soccer games, but the Jewish children would not let themselves be pushed around. In the ensuing name-calling, I would often hear, "Jews, go to Palestine!"

Among the adolescents and university students who were on vacation for the summer, quarrels broke out at the local swimming hole on the Liwiec River. This was a public area. We went in groups to the river, and often young Christians would come over to us in the river and tell us to move on, that they wanted to swim there. We protested, "There is enough room here for everyone. Why do you want this spot?" They retorted, "This is our place." Again, they would tell us to go to Palestine. Then they would throw stones, so we left the water and threw stones. Sometimes several boys required stitches. We all accepted this as part of life. Jews always had to fight to protect their rights. It seemed, though, that a single Christian boy and I could be friends and talk on a personal level, provided we were alone. If there were a group, then the Christians and Jews separated and there was always friction.

Some of the Polish farmers were crude, coarse people. Alcoholism was a constant problem, and I heard many farm wives complain that their husbands frequently drank too much and beat them. All the farm people in the area would be invited whenever any of the farmers hosted a wedding. Often, the celebration got out of hand and ended in tragedy. Some young hothead would die in a knife fight. The undertaker would come by the next day to buy lumber for the coffin and gossip about the details.

At fourteen, I enrolled in a small yeshiva. For the following five years, I studied in the morning and then after lunch worked in our store and lumberyard until evening. We conducted business freely with non-Jews and had few problems. They liked to buy from us because we were able to sell goods more cheaply than our Christian counterparts. Centuries of experience had made Jews better and more competitive businessmen. Jewish professionals—doctors, lawyers, dentists—were perceived as better than the gentile professionals. Professional schools maintained unofficial quotas, and only the best Jewish applicants gained entrance. So Christians, despite the inbred anti-Semitism, preferred the services of Jewish professionals.

Why the deep-seated suspicion? The Polish gentiles, almost all Roman Catholic, had been inculcated with anti-Jewish views for centuries. Over the years, the Christian forgot that they had welcomed the Jews to Poland and had provided a haven against persecution of the Jews during the Middle Ages. In my time, priests constantly preached that the Jews were responsible for the death of Jesus. Near Easter these anti-Semitic ravings were especially virulent.

In fact, the Romans were responsible for the crucifixion of Jesus. The Vatican recently acknowledged this after years of misunderstanding and prejudice. The Romans during Jesus's time had conquered most of the civilized world and used slavery and oppression to keep their empire intact. Jesus was popular among the Jews and preached to them, stirring their passions. The Romans feared a rebellion in Israel, an uprising that might spread through the rest of the empire, so they fabricated charges against Jesus and crucified him with the blessing of a few coerced Jews.

Over the centuries, history was distorted. For hundreds of years, priests told their congregants that Jews used the blood of slaughtered Christian children to make matzos, unleavened bread that Jews eat on Passover to recall when the ancient Hebrew slaves left Egypt in freedom. Matzo is made from water and flour. Ancient Hebrews sacrificed sheep and goats to God thousands of years ago, but the notion that Jews would use human blood in any religious ceremony is utter nonsense. These concepts derived from medieval prejudices that were fanned by ignorance and fear.

One summer, a few years before the outbreak of World War II, I was walking alongside a wagon loaded with freshly cut lumber on one of our weekly trips to the forests. We had purchased trees from a farmer, had transported them by horse and wagon to the community sawmill, and were taking the cut lumber back to the lumberyard. We did not want to overtax our horse, so the hired man and I walked alongside the wagon on the dirt road. We passed many small farmhouses. At one point, we saw a group of small children, three to six years old, playing in front of a house. Suddenly I heard one of them scream, "A Jew is coming! He is going to get us!" They quickly disappeared into the house.

I was not surprised. Jews were depicted to Catholic children from early childhood as bogymen. To keep children from running into the streets, Poles didn't tell them that they might be hit by a cart or a galloping horse. They told them that a Jew would get them.

We could be identified easily because we dressed differently. The Christians, farmers for the most part, wore work clothes. Living in towns and working in businesses, the Jews dressed well and were conspicuous in the country. Some religious Jews wore long, black coats and round-brimmed black hats and had long, curly sideburns. Often, they wore *tallises* (prayer shawls) underneath their shirts, in keeping with the precepts of the Torah.

The 1930s brought not only a worldwide Depression, but also terrible trials for our family, especially my mother. One cool autumn day, my father traveled to a nearby farm to oversee logging operations. When we needed lumber to sell, we paid a farmer to allow us to cut the trees on his property. My father had to be there to make sure that the workers took trees with straight trunks or the materials would be useless. Boards must be straight. He fell asleep after the day's work. When he awoke, he was covered with dew and developed a chill. A cough resulted that did not respond to medication. Medical attention could be haphazard in those days, and my father was in his fifties. The cough never left. He became progressively weaker and finally died in 1934. By this time my older brother, Yitzchak, had married and moved to another part of town. This left me as the eldest male at home and at age eighteen, I became head of the household.

Chapter 2

Gathering Storm Clouds

I

With no natural geographical border defenses, such as lakes or mountains, to protect it from invasion, Poland has always been susceptible to military intervention by its European neighbors. Weak Polish leaders squabbled in the eighteenth century, undermining the country's central government and exposing Poland to foreign invasion. Russia, Austria, and Germany all gobbled up parts of the country. Throughout the nineteenth century, Poland no longer appeared on maps. After World War I, the Allies agreed to allow the Poles to create a new republic with a democratic, parliamentary government. After so many years, there was once again a sovereign Poland. But Marshal Pilsudski, minister of war, almost immediately violated the spirit of the new constitution by establishing dictatorial control. He died in 1935. A series of weak leaders followed. When war broke out, Poland once again lost its status as an independent, sovereign nation, as Germany and the Soviet Union each claimed control of portions of the country.

Adolf Hitler rose to power in Germany in 1933. After World War I ended in 1918, the German economy collapsed. The democratic government could not continue meeting the huge reparations payments heaped on Germany by the victorious Allies and still maintain a viable economy. Inflation made the Deutschmark worthless, and the average

German saw his life savings wiped out in a short time. The failing economic and political situation caused people to panic. Germany polarized as citizens looked to extremist parties to solve their problems—usually the Communists or the National Socialists (Nazis).

The Wall Street stock market crash in 1929 and the worldwide economic Depression that followed exacerbated Germany's woes, polarizing voters even more. Hitler, an unsuccessful artist from a small town in Austria and a corporal during World War I, became head of the Nazi Party in 1920. It had been a small workers' party, but he re-directed its policies. It became a right-wing, bigoted, super-nationalist voice for a few members of the lower and middle classes. The party grew and became quite successful in the early years of the Depression. Hitler was appointed a compromise chancellor in 1933, though the Nazis did not control a majority of the seats in the parliament. Wealthy aristocrats and influential politicians hoped Hitler would bring order. Once the political scene had calmed, they reasoned, they would get rid of him. Hitler surprised the nobility and the political power brokers in Germany with his ruthlessness and political cunning. He mesmerized the German people with false promises of glory and with state-sponsored jobs; his popularity soared. The Nazis then consolidated power by intimidating or murdering all opposition, and Hitler became the sole political force in Germany by 1934.

He revived the German economy with an intense military buildup, with public works projects, with a reorganized economy, and by seizing all the wealth and property owned by Jews and some other minorities. Hitler believed and convinced many of the German people that they belonged to a superior race, the Aryans—a supposed ancient tribe of blue-eyed, blond people, who the Nazis claimed were larger physically and more intelligent than other peoples. Actually, social historians have found that no such single tribe of people ever existed. On the basis of this mythical superior race, Hitler inflated the self-importance of the German people. Hitler and his party propagandists tried to convince Germans that other peoples were inferior, and that it was the obligation of the new German nation to free Germanic peoples in other countries.

To this end, the Saarland to the west of Germany near France voted in January 1935 to join Germany. Hitler marched into the Rhineland, which is adjacent to Germany and east of Belgium and the Netherlands, in March 1936, violating the terms of the Versailles agreement reached after World War I. France and Great Britain did not make a move. Emboldened, the Nazis called for a plebiscite in Austria in March 1938, and the Austrians voted overwhelmingly to join Germany's Third Reich. British Prime Minister Neville Chamberlain met with Hitler in Munich in September 1938, and after their meeting, the Sudetenland of Czechoslovakia was ceded to Germany. Bohemia, Moravia, and Memel in Lithuania soon joined the Third Reich. Almost all German-speaking people lived under Nazi domination. But Hitler had only whetted his appetite. More would follow.

The Jews of Wegrow knew what Hitler stood for, but we could never have imagined what he would accomplish eventually. Encouraged by the successes of fascism in Germany and Italy, many young Poles turned to bullying tactics in the late 1930s. The level of anti-Semitism nationwide gradually increased. More and more anti-Jewish propaganda appeared in newspapers.

In November of 1938 we heard of the events of *Kristallnacht* in Germany. Gangs of Nazis in "spontaneous demonstrations" ordered by Propaganda Minister Joseph Goebbels burned synagogues, destroyed Jewish businesses and shops, and beat and murdered several Jews. Large numbers of German Jews were sent to concentration camps. In Hitler's twisted mind, the Jews were responsible for all the Germans' problems. He believed that Germany had been stabbed in the back by Jews, resulting in the Allied victory in World War I. He also claimed that Jews formed an international business and banking conspiracy that was responsible for Germany's financial problems. Jews were the lowest of all races, the Nazis argued. In fact, Hitler believed Jews to be subhuman and unworthy of citizenship or of even the right to mix with the German people. The Nazis passed a series of laws that allowed the government to take away all Jewish property and possessions, to deny Jews citizenship, to prohibit Jews from traveling or living in certain areas, to remove Jews from nearly all jobs, and eventually to segregate Jews and Christians, so that Jews could be easily taken away in the night to concentration camps.

The Polish Jews were horrified. Each began to think of how to prepare for the future, should the wave of heightened anti-Semitism spread. Many planned to leave for other countries, but no place would accept them. The only immediate possibility was to emigrate illegally to Palestine, an alternative chosen by many of my friends. It was a very difficult undertaking requiring forged papers, dangerous passage on leaky ships, and finally a desperate dash ashore to beaches heavily patrolled by British soldiers in Palestine. Some succeeded, but others were sent back or killed.

In the United States, after World War I, Congress imposed stringent immigration quotas, because ethnocentric voters feared foreign influence and an influx of workers, who would take jobs from American citizens. It was extremely difficult to get a visa to emigrate to the United States from Eastern Europe in the 1920s and 1930s. Everyone wanted to go to America, but anyone with any hope of success needed a sponsor—someone living in the United States who would handle the paperwork and guarantee the applicant a job and a place to live. Even then, the wait could be ten years or more. I had an uncle in Oakland, California, with whom I corresponded regularly. I pleaded often in my letters for him to sponsor my family, but he never answered those pleas.

Nevertheless, I felt that someday we might have to leave Poland, and so I began to plan for that possibility. Using the profits from our store, I exchanged Polish zlotys for gold coins. I was careful not to do this in Wegrow, where everyone would know what I was doing. I feared robbers would come looking for the gold, if word leaked. Instead, I went to the main government-operated bank in Warsaw, where it was likely I would not be recognized. I could purchase gold coins there without attracting attention.

I exchanged zlotys for American five-, ten-, and twenty-dollar gold pieces and Russian gold coins in denominations of five and ten rubles. Then, I stored the coins in metal containers and buried the boxes underground in the closed sheds at the back of our property. Between 1934 and 1939, I converted most of our earnings into gold, about $4,000, which was a considerable sum in the 1930s.

As news of German atrocities spread, Poles turned increasingly hostile toward Jews. In 1938, the federal government introduced the *numerus clausus*, which restricted the entrance of Jews into universities. Later, Polish students demanded segregated seating for Jewish students in the college lecture halls. Gangs beat and knifed Jewish students. Outside the universities, young Poles organized boycotts of businesses owned by Jews. Jewish representatives to the Polish Parliament protested. An unsympathetic, anti-Semitic minister of the interior, Skladkowsky, told these emissaries that such attacks were improper, but boycotts were entirely acceptable. Soon, young Poles, usually aged 15 to 35, began picketing Jewish business establishments all over the country. Wearing black berets and armed with sticks, they prevented non-Jews from entering, telling them that the Jews would defraud them. If the customer shopped there anyway, these hooligans placed a drawing of a pig on his back when he emerged.

Polish police were stationed near stores and businesses to keep order, but they frequently sided with the young toughs. Often, the picketers who pummeled Jews claimed that they had been attacked first and were merely defending themselves. We witnessed many attacks first hand, because our building was in the center of town, facing the marketplace.

Once, while I was standing at the window of the store, a group of picketers carrying sticks entered and dragged me into the street, threatening to kill me. They claimed that I had taunted them with an iron rod. A nearby policeman saved me.

Such was life in the late 1930s. Day by day, Jews abandoned their stores and gave up their livelihoods, while Christians opened their own businesses nearby. Boycotts were directed against Jewish doctors, lawyers, and other professionals.

Hitler decided that the German people needed more "living space." He looked east to Poland, where he figured the inferior Slavs could be enslaved or relocated to allow more room for Germanic people. In late August 1939, Hitler and the Soviet leader, Josef Stalin, signed the Pact of Nonaggression in which both sides agreed not to go to war with each other. It was then decided that the two nations would invade and divide Poland, reclaiming land that was given back to the Poles after World War I—Germany from the west and the Soviets, two weeks later, from the east.

First, though, the Nazis, who were always cognizant of world opinion, needed a pretext. They transported several inmates from a concentration camp and dressed them in Polish soldiers' uniforms. These inmates "seized" a radio station in Germany just inside the Polish border. The "soldiers" announced to German listeners that the Poles controlled the station. The Nazis killed the phoney soldiers and left the bodies to be found in the Polish uniforms. On this pretext, Germany invaded Poland on September 1, 1939.

II

I was awakened early that day by a frightened neighbor, who brought news of the invasion. I dressed quickly and went outside. A radio blared in the marketplace. Jewish men, women, and children stood listening to the reports, and I saw despair and horror on hundreds of faces.

In the United States, the year before this, a radio drama show had broadcast a false report that Martians were invading New Jersey. It was actually a science fiction radio program, "The War of the Worlds," but listeners were told only before and after the program that the broadcast was just a dramatization. Thousands of people in New Jersey did not hear the disclaimers and were frightened beyond belief, flooding the network switchboard with phone calls and fleeing their homes in panic. They feared an unknown enemy. They could not even have imagined the fear we felt in early September 1939. These were not Martians, but Germans, and what we might expect from them would be at least as terrible, and more certain, than what the Martians would have done to people in New Jersey.

The radio reports that morning announced that Hitler's army had invaded the country in great strength, that the Poles were resisting valiantly, and that all reservists should be prepared for active duty. I was of military age and I stood ready to fight, but I did not know to whom I should report or where I should go. As it turned out, the fighting ended almost as soon as it had begun.

On September 2, the war intensified. The Germans attacked in great force with tanks and artillery along the entire front. They outnumbered the Poles by two to one on land and ten to one in the air. The Germans had eighty-six infantry, six tank, and eight mechanized divisions. In the air, the Luftwaffe could marshal 1,174 fighters and 1,516 bombers. The Poles had 30 infantry divisions, 300 light tanks, 154 fighter planes, and 159 bombers. Often, the Poles rode on horseback against armored divisions of tanks, trucks, and jeeps. It was hopeless. England and France declared war on Germany, and World War II was underway.

I considered what I could do to save our family and belongings. I packed store merchandise in wooden crates and buried the containers in the lumberyard under the dirt floors of the open sheds. In so doing, I hoped to prevent loss of all my goods from looting. In the next two days, I managed to bury about half the merchandise.

On September 4 the Germans bombed Warsaw incessantly. Tall, sturdy buildings were reduced to rubble, and thousands of civilians were killed. Most of the bombings was concentrated in the crowded Jewish neighborhoods. German-speaking spies had been working inside Poland for years, and their reports permitted the Nazis to plan all their aerial attacks to kill as many Jews as possible. Polish radio optimistically reported that the Poles had repulsed the Germans and that reservists should stand by. Property owners were ordered to store boxes of sand and tanks of water in attics for fighting fires that might result from bomb attacks.

We feared for our safety in Wegrow, so we closed our home and store, and on September 5 we traveled eighteen miles to a small farm village near Jarnic. A farmer there had traded with us, and we trusted him. That evening, the entire family slept on hay in the barn. It was still warm, and we lived without great discomfort in the barn for a week. We did not know it then, but this was the first of our numerous "homes" where we hid over the next five years.

On September 7 radio reports revealed that not only had Warsaw been captured, but also Wegrow. This frightened us, but the farm remained quiet, and we did not panic.

Yet, we needed to know what this meant to us, so a few days later we asked our host to travel to Wegrow to learn what he could about the town and our possessions. He returned the same evening with bad news. The Germans, in full uniform and carrying machine guns, had overrun Wegrow. Upon arriving, they rounded up all Jews and herded them into the town square, ordering them to keep their hands held high above their heads, as if they were criminals. The German commander ordered the Jews to obey all German edicts. He pointed to a *Volksdeutsch* (ethnic German) from Wegrow and said that man would be the new mayor. The Jews were told to follow his orders.

The new mayor, about 40, was a local high school teacher. He and his wife frequented our store, and I had thought that he was a decent fellow. Later, I learned that he had spied for the Nazis for years.

Our farmer friend also told us that the windows in our store and our house had been smashed, the doors knocked in, and the merchandise looted. We decided to go home.

When we crept into town, we saw streets filled with goose-stepping German soldiers. Armored German vehicles incessantly rumbled over the ancient stone streets as they passed through town. At least 2,000 soldiers were stationed in Wegrow. In the store, empty boxes lay on the floor, the clothing missing from them. All over the floor lay goose-down lining, all that was left from shredded bedspreads. Furniture had been hacked to pieces. We repaired the windows and doors, boarded up the store, and slept on the floor that night.

In the morning, the new mayor stopped by. When he surveyed the destruction and saw my mother weeping, he seemed to feel a little guilty.

"I am sorry, but you can see that the war brings no good," he said to my mother. Turning to me, he asked, "Will you sell me two shirts for my brother? He has come from Germany to live with me."

"I don't know if I have any shirts left. You see what has happened here. I will try to find some and let you know in a few days." I could not tell anyone about the buried merchandse, particularly not someone appointed mayor by the Nazis.

Just then, the door burst open and a tall German soldier swaggered in carrying a dagger. He grabbed me by the throat, placed the dagger at my heart, and demanded, "You give me some shirts and trousers. Now! Or I'll end your filthy little life!" I told him I didn't have any. I thought the end had come.

Fortunately, the mayor interceded. "Excuse me, I am the new mayor here, and I came to buy some shirts, too. But you see that the store has been looted." Walking around the disheveled shop, he told the soldier, "I believe him when he says that he has no merchandise available. I have known him for many years and I know that he would not lie."

"I'm sorry," the soldier said. He then grabbed a raw egg from the table, made a small hole in the shell with his dagger, and sucked the contents down noisily. He threw away the shell and left. This was our first encounter with the end of civilized life as we knew it. Looters, murderers, and opportunists would control our destinies for years to come.

The color returned to my face. I felt as if I had risen from the dead. If the mayor had not been there, the soldier would have stabbed me.

The mayor departed quietly, and my sister walked outside to see what was going on. She returned quickly and told me to hide, because the Germans were looking for men to fill work details. Workers were taken away, and many never returned.

The Germans set a 5:00 P.M. curfew for Jews. I hid in the attic, but I was so frightened that I could not sleep at all that night. Again the next day, I did not leave the house and Menucha went out to survey the city. Soldiers circulated in trucks, looking for Jewish men for forced labor, but they did not take women.

That day, a husky civilian came to the store carrying over his shoulder a large burlap sack stuffed with clothing. I was in the shop, and when he noticed me, he grabbed my shirt front, pulled me toward him, and in German ordered me to take off my trousers. He wanted them. My mother said, "Come with me to the closet and I'll give you better trousers." He released me and I sprinted through the doorway. He gave chase, but with the heavy sack, he could not catch me. Then, he took whatever he could from the house and left. We had to guard constantly against looters. I knew we would not be able to keep anything in the store on display, until some order returned.

On the third day after our return to town, military transports filled with soldiers arrived at the lumberyard.

An officer said, "We are confiscating all your supplies. The lumber is needed to repair bombed bridges. You are to help load the lumber. Under no circumstances remove or sell any lumber. Disobey these orders and you will all be killed."

There was no point in trying to replenish the lumberyard supplies. The Germans would simply come and confiscate the wood again. We were out of the lumber business.

I could not remain in our house. We were visible in the center of town and, at any time, someone could draft me for labor. Because my brother Yitzchak lived on Sokolover Street near the edge of town where few Jews lived, I figured the Germans would not comb that neighborhood looking for Jewish laborers. When he had married several years prior to the war, my brother moved in with his in-laws in a Christian neighborhood. The family was Jewish, but could not find a house in a Jewish neighborhood, since housing was scarce in Europe in those days, and often a family passed ownership of a house on for generations. This family and my brother lived in a Christian neighborhood, because this was where the family had acquired a house. They would have preferred to live in a Jewish section, but had to settle for what was available. In this case, it worked to our advantage. My mother and Menucha stayed home with Moshe, who remained out of sight, and I left to stay with Yitzchak. Yerachmiel had moved in with his girlfriend's family.

On the first day at Yitzchak's, as we sat in the house, we heard someone

pounding at the front door and shouting in German, "*Raus! Raus!* (Out!)"
My sister-in-law opened the door. Two SS men carrying machine guns
collared Yitzchak and me and forced us outside, kicking us with their
heavy boots as we walked. They told us to raise our hands and line up
in front of the house. The SS was an elite Nazi guard in charge of civilian
control in occupied countries. Mostly, they carried out Hitler's vendetta
against the Jews by identifying Jewish citizens and separating them from
the rest of the population. Eventually, the SS carried out the mass killings.
They were selected for their unswerving loyalty to the Nazis and for
their brutal natures.

In the street we saw many other Jews already standing with their arms
raised above their heads. Across the street, soldiers pointed machine
guns at us, ready to shoot us down at the slightest provocation. So much
for my theory about the SS not visiting Christian neighborhoods! The
SS men asked whether we had any weapons and searched us. They found
nothing. They did not seem to know what to do then, so they asked one
of their officers, who told us to leave but to be ready for a work detail
at any time. I'm not certain why they rounded us up, but I was so terrified
that I could not lower my arms. Dazed, I went back into the house arms
still raised, where it took some time for me to revover. Once more I had
thought I would die.

For several days, I hid at my brother's house as the SS searched for
Jews. Then, Jews from other towns began appearing in Wegrow, as the
Germans sought to build up the Jewish labor force in the area. In the
latter years of the war, many Christian Poles from other areas were also
forced into labor gangs, but I never saw any Christians in Wegrow abused
in this way. In 1939 and 1940, the Germans were satisfied with working
the Jews at heavy labor without pay.

III

From Wegrow, the main road to Warsaw wended through the towns of
Kaluszyn, Minsk Mazowiecki, Milosna, and Praga before reaching the
capital city. The iron bridge over the Vistula River marked the eastern
boundary of Warsaw. German transports moved soldiers, supplies, and
weapons over the dusty road that wound through Wegrow and these
other towns as they advanced toward the border that separated the Soviet
and German occupation areas. In the coming years, transports would
take a different route with a different cargo. About fifty miles east of
Wegrow was the town of Siedlce. Near here, in an area of forests and
farms, the infamous Treblinka concentration camp was built, where Jews
were killed from the spring of 1941 until the autumn of 1944. Eventually,

almost all the Jews from Wegrow died at Treblinka, having been trans-
ported by open trucks over the unpaved road to Siedlce. The road to
Warsaw had been a route of commerce and salvation for the Jews of
Wegrow. Now, it would become the road to the gas chambers. The
Germans and the Poles would destroy the Jews of Wegrow, but they
took their time. First, they tried to destroy our pride and our culture.

Wegrow had a large synagogue 'complex. The largest building contained the synagogue, which was about 200 years old and constructed
of solid-brick walls two feet thick. Inside was a magnificent, forty-foot-
high domed ceiling covered with intricate murals painted by one of the
foremost European artists of the eighteenth century. They depicted
scenes from the Torah. The front of the Holy Ark was intricately carved
into the shape of two large lions and plated in gold. In the center of the
sanctuary, a large platform waited for the reading of the Torah. Upon
the *bema* (raised platform) were three large upholstered chairs used for
ritual circumcisions. At the rear of the room, a balcony for women
worshipers overlooked the sanctuary. Women sit separately from men
in Orthodox synagogues. They do not participate directly in the service,
except to follow the readings and chant when the congregation, as a
whole, chants. Most European Jews were Orthodox, though most American Jews today are not. At the southern end of the synagogue was a
small chapel where the craftsmen held their own services. As a boy, I
sat in wonder in this synagogue filled with history and the word of God.
Its magnificence washed over me, leaving me in awe and reminding me
how important it was to be a Jew.

Near the synagogue was a house of study called the Old Bais Midrash.
Seven hundred years old with walls of brick three feet thick and doors
of iron, it was the oldest strucure in town. About 150 feet away stood a
building known as the New Bais Midrash, larger than the older house
of study, and about 200 years old. The town *mikva* (the ritual bath) was
about 250 feet from the main synagogue. Married Jewish women im-
mersed themselves there to purify themselves for the Sabbath.

In addition to the Great Synagogue court, there were several other
houses of study, in other parts of town. One was Reb Hillel's Bais Midrash, where traveling rabbis frequently delivered their sermons. Another
was Reb Hirsch Yechiel's Bais Midrash. There were many Hasidic *shtie-
blach* (small meeting and discussion centers) in Poland, one for each of
the different Hasidic groups, including the Gerer, Aleksander, Kotzker,
Radziner, Sokolower, Hamshenower, Hamener, and Sochaczewer.

There was one rabbi for the entire town. He was chosen by the Jewish
community. The rabbi had an assistant religious judge, called the *moreh
horaah*, who acted as a mediator of disputes among Jewish residents so
that Jews rarely involved themselves in civil court actions. Our town's
rabbi was Jacob Mendel Morgenstern, the son of the rabbi of Sokolow.

At the outbreak of the war, the Nazis closed down all synagogues in Poland and allowed no open Jewish worship. The synagogues sat idle, and all this splendor that had been built up over hundreds of years was now denied to us.

Still, the Jewish community had a common cause. Jews founded a small hospital to care for emergency injury cases. It was staffed by Jewish doctors, nurses, and hospital aides. The duties of the last group included getting patients to the hospital and supervising sanitary conditions. Patients who needed bathing were taken to the mikva. Usually, the mikva was for only ritual bathing, but Jews are practical about emergencies. My brother, Moshe, was a member of the sanitation squad during the time that I was at Yitzchak's house.

In these early days of the invasion, many wealthy Jews were arrested and taken to the church. Among them was Wladek Satenstein, owner of the electric power station and the sawmill, and the wealthiest Jew in town. He was not religious and, in fact, knew little about Judaism. The Nazis did not care who was religious and who was not. In fact, Catholics who were thought to have had a Jewish grandparent were considered Jews by the Nazis and treated accordingly. The Germans held the town's wealthy Jews for several days and finally took them away. They never returned. This provided a convenient, "legal" way for the Germans to confiscate much of the wealth of the town. It was a curse to be a wealthy Jew in Poland in September 1939.

The High Holy Days, Rosh Hashanah and Yom Kippur, were approaching, but all synagogues had been closed. The Germans chose Yom Kippur to make a point. Soldiers came to the rabbi's home, where he sat praying in his long silk coat. The SS ordered him to put on the velvet hat which he customarily wore on Yom Kippur. Then they took him from his home and dragged him to the open marketplace near the horses and wagons of the peasants, who had come to town to shop. They gave him a broom and made him sweep. He was ordered to put the debris and horse manure into his velvet hat and take it to the central garbage dump. He did as they ordered, continuing until he had finished cleaning the entire marketplace.

Then the Germans came nearer to the rabbi and told him to undress. He removed his overcoat and his *tallis katan*, the fringed prayer garment which he always wore. Without warning, a soldier drove a bayonet into his belly. The rabbi screamed horribly and fell to the ground. My mother, who had been standing outside our house, witnessed all this. She tried to run to the rabbi, but they held her back. The Jewish nurses came and took the rabbi to the provisional Jewish hospital, where he died the next morning.

The Nazis chose Yom Kippur to send a message. Our God meant nothing and on the Day of Atonement, when all lives are sealed in the

Book of Life for the next year, the Germans sealed the rabbi's fate. If any Jew in Wegrow had previously had doubts about what the Nazis had in mind for him the following year, he should have known that day.

The funeral was small, because Jews were afraid to participate. The great rabbi of Wegrow was laid to rest amid a terrible fear that had descended upon the entire community. He had the dignity of a funeral. Maybe he was lucky.

Daily, new Germans appeared in town, and soldiers dragged Jews away for forced labor. Most of this time I remained in hiding at Yitzchak's house. In October the Germans summoned leaders of our Jewish community and ordered the formation of a local Jewish government, a *Judenrat*, with a president and a vice-president. A similar *Judenrat* had been established in September in Warsaw. No one wanted to be president, but someone had to comply with the Germans' orders. Finally, Mordechai Zajman, a rabbi's son, was chosen. Shmuel Halberstat served as vice-president, Abraham Yeshaieh Weintraub as chairman of the Labor Committee, and Yitzchak Kozuch as vice-chairman of that committee. They also formed a Jewish police force and a housing authority.

The *Judenrat* had the power to tax, to draft Jews for labor, and to move people from one house to another. The Jewish police wore dark blue uniforms with arm bands for identification. They carried rubber billy clubs but were not given arms. If the Jewish police were not obeyed, they could get help from the Polish police, who did carry arms.

The Jews obeyed German orders through the auspices of the Jewish president, who either enforced rules or faced execution. The Germans delegated authority and had to do little except mete out brutal punishment to set examples. The Germans ordered that all Jewish businesses be reopened or the stores would be given to the Poles. Taxes were to be paid to the Germans. In this way, an efficient system allowed the Germans to rely on others to supply free labor, to collect tribute, and to keep track of all the Jews in town. They had only to demand, and others took care of the details.

Hearing the new orders, I decided I had to leave Yitzchak's house and put the business back in order. I unburied some merchandise from beneath the sheds and replaced it in the store. It did not take long for eager buyers to empty the store. Another crate of merchandise also disappeared quickly. Soon all the merchandise was sold. All the buyers were gentiles. Jews knew that anything they bought would be seized by the Germans.

Jews from other towns continued to flood Wegrow. Eventually, most wound up in the ghetto in Warsaw. Many came from Lodz. Those who were not transferred remained confined in the ghetto of Lodz, the second largest city in Poland with about 750,000 people. Lodz was a manufacturing center with many factories. Perhaps 80 percent of these factories belonged to Jews, my father used to tell me. He had relatives in a small town near Lodz. Similarly, Jews were evicted from Piotrkow, Aleksandrow, Pultusk, Wyszkow, Kaluszyn, and other cities. By the end of the first year of the war, there were about 16,000 Jews in Wegrow, where there had been 6,000 before.

The housing authority ordered that all Jews who had more than a kitchen and one bedroom had to give the remaining rooms to other Jews. We took in a family of five, for which we received no rent. The transferees had little money and few possessions, because they had been forced to leave nearly everything behind. Each person could take only one suitcase. All homes in Wegrow became crowded, and Jews became progressively poorer. Day by day, conditions worsened.

The German authorities then ordered every Jew living in a house or an apartment to pay monthly rent or be evicted. The Germans brought two *Volksdeutschen* from Silesia to Wegrow to set up a rent bureau. They surveyed each house, assigning rent payments. When they came into my house I chatted with them and got to know them. They seemed to be decent people. I packed two shirts for each of them from the business and offered them as a sign of friendship. They thanked me profusely, and later we were assessed a lower rent than we would have had to pay otherwise. This was the beginning of a long series of bribes and payments, which we kept up during the entire war.

The demands had only begun. The *Judenrat* compiled a list of all Jewish households and individuals of working age. I hid and was not among the 200 chosen that time. The German police marched the selected workers twenty-five miles to a freight terminal in the town of Przezadka, near Sokolow. When the men came home after a day of labor, their faces swollen from beatings, they could barely walk. They had been given neither water nor food all day. Much of the work involved transferring sacks of wheat weighing 110 pounds each, while the Germans stood over them striking them with truncheons and kicking them with heavy boots.

The next day the police demanded 250 Jews. The *Judenrat* complied. These men met the same fate. Every day, the work list grew. Young Jewish men became exhausted from the labor and the beatings.

Jewish police by night invaded Jewish homes and dragged young men out to fill the labor quotas. My brother Moshe and I slept in the attic during the night and hid in the outhouse during the day. We also had to be careful to avoid busy streets when we moved about.

The *Judenrat* was in a difficult position. Because it could not provide the numbers demanded by the Germans, it began to negotiate for smaller numbers. It bribed the Germans with gifts of fur coats and diamonds for their wives, and fancy boots for the men. But the demands abated only temporarily. The *Judenrat* levied higher and higher taxes on the Jewish community, attempting to raise more money to bribe the German police.

Conditions were bad, particularly for those who had been driven from their homes. Filthy, emaciated people wandered about in rags begging for scraps and a warm place to curl up. They sought odd jobs, even as substitute workers for the labor force. If a Jewish home were required to contribute a worker, it could hire a destitute Jew as a substitute. This situation endured for a long time. I continued to operate the store in an attempt to pay taxes levied by the Germans for living in our own house, to pay taxes levied by the *Judenrat* to buy substitute workers, and to provide for our daily living expenses. I had to keep out of sight most of the time, however, or I would be dragged away. I had to stay away from the Germans. At any time, a soldier could become annoyed with a Jew and beat him to death or split his face open with the butt of a gun. No one would say anything. No one would do anything. The Germans had a license to kill any Jew for any reason, and I knew it.

IV

When my stock of merchandise ran low, I decided to journey to Warsaw to purchase more. Jews had to travel by open freight truck. We stood in the bed of the truck, packed together like cattle. I had a permit or I would not have been allowed to leave. When I arrived in Warsaw, I was shocked. Many tall brick and steel buildings that had dotted the Warsaw skyline had been reduced to rubble by German bombing raids. Long streets of modern buildings and apartment houses were in ruins. Heaps of brick, steel, and cement rubble marked every block. German soldiers patrolled everywhere.

I sought out the wholesalers from whom I had purchased my merchandise in the past. They were fine, respectable people. Before the war, I used to enjoy the business trips to Warsaw. Merchandise was kept in huge crates in warehouses. I would tell the wholesalers what I needed— colors, styles, sizes, and amounts—and they would show me samples from the crates. I would strike a deal and have the material shipped to Wegrow. Now I searched in vain for them for two days. Many people had been killed in bombing raids. Others had been shot by the Germans or taken away, never to be seen again. Just as in Wegrow, the wealthy Jews had been taken first.

Mournful and depressed people roamed the streets shuffling through the rubble. No one in a modern, peaceful society can imagine the boundless pain and suffering. Every fifteen to twenty minutes a group of people would emerge from a ruined buildings and run through the streets shouting "Escape, they are drafting for labor!" I followed a regular routine of hiding among the ruins of brick and iron scrap and then venturing out again when it became quiet. Over and over again, this occurred until a whole day passed. By nightfall, I grew tired of searching and sought out the home of my brother's wife's sister. Her family had lived in Warsaw for some time and I always slept there when I visited. After the German invasion, I brought them a little money each time so that they could get some extra food.

Sleep would not come. Visions of my prewar friends, the merchants and wealthy people, passed before my eyes. It seeemed that no one was left. The world had turned into a hellish graveyard, where only ragged zombies screamed, "Escape! Escape!" Where was the proud, elegant Warsaw of only a few weeks ago? What happened to the peaceful land where grain waved in the wind and gentle streams gurgled past immense forests? I was twenty-three years old and should have been enjoying my youth, selecting a bride, and making plans for the future. I couldn't think of anything except how to get from one day to the next. Hell did not have burning fires and creatures with long tails and pitchforks. Hell was on earth and I was living there.

The next day I resumed my search. I learned that Jews had arrived in Warsaw from Lodz. Bombs had destroyed many Jewish neighbor-hoods, so few of these new arrivals had places to live. Thousands of people wandered the streets looking for bread or food scraps.

I never found my former friends. Eventually, I made some new con-nections and was able to buy the merchandise for which I had come. These Jews in the ghetto arranged for the merchandise to be shipped back to Wegrow by Poles. The merchandise was taken to trucks outside the ghetto, where it was transferred to another truck headed for We-grow. In the months to come, the Warsaw ghetto Jews showed amazing ingenuity in their fight to stay alive. For instance, when my contacts ran out of regular stock, they improvised by making sheets and pillowcases into shirts. They dyed the sheets and sewed buttons onto the material. The clothing was not perfect, but supplies everywhere were so tight that buyers were grateful to obtain any sort of clothing. Once the Jews in the ghetto were sealed in by a wall, they threw the merchandise over the wall into waiting trucks.

I returned home, extremely depressed, but at least with merchandise to replenish my store's supplies and keep the Germans from confiscating our business.

V

Now, I had to find a permanent plan for avoiding the labor draft. The outhouse was several hundred feet behind our house and was surrounded by a vegetable garden about fifteen feet wide and twenty-five feet long. A six-foot-high fence with a padlocked gate surrounded the garden. To use the outhouse, we would unlock the padlock, open the gate, and go into the garden. My mother and sister would sit in front of the house as lookouts, and when they saw the Germans grabbing people for work, they would go into the house and alert Moshe and me. We would hide in the outhouse, and Menucha would then lock the gate from the outside. We sat in our foul-smelling quarters for hours at a time. We dared not leave until someone told us it was safe. At night, we were forced to hide elsewhere: the attic, a shed, or another house where there were no able-bodied men to be forced into labor.

I grew weary of running from one hiding place to another. Winter was approaching, and it would soon become difficult to hide outside for hours at a time. I developed a plan for a permanent hiding place. By this time the family of five who had been living with us had moved to another city, so our family lived alone in the house.

The back of our store opened into the kitchen, which provided access to the rest of the house. An attic extended over the store and the kitchen. It could be reached through a small hatch in the kitchen ceiling. The attic was twenty feet wide, thirteen feet long, and four feet high in front, slanting downward from there to meet the floor in back.

I decided to build a false wall in the attic perpendicular to the front wall so that we could hide behind the wall in an area that was six feet wide and thirteen feet long. I made the wall using brick left over from the reconstruction of the front of the building. That part of the building had been destroyed by fire in 1937, and I had rebuilt it. Brick was left over from the job. I made a two-foot-wide brick door in the middle of the wall just large enough for one person to crawl through. The door was framed by an iron strip four inches wide and one-quarter inch thick and was hinged to the wall. It opened into the hiding place. Obviously, it was important that this door could not be recognized. I hid one edge behind the chimney and the other behind a false chimney which I built in front of it. The top of the door was buried behind a rafter, and the bottom was obscured by a layer of straw and clay used for insulation. From the inside of the hiding place the door could be braced closed with a length of two-by-four lumber.

Because no one, Jew or gentile, could know of my plans, I had to use only the leftover bricks and work at night for several days. I was lucky that I needed no outside help. If anyone had known of this hiding place, no one in my family would have survived.

After completing the masonry work, I made a thick rope ladder with sturdy sticks for rungs and attached a length of two-by-four to one end to weight the rope down for climbing. The rope remained in the attic, out of sight. Such a ladder would arouse suspicion, if left out. To obtain the ladder, we placed the kitchen table under the attic hatch and reached in for the rope. In the hiding place we stored dried bread, cookies, water, and sugar, so that we could retreat to this annex quickly and not need to leave for days. It might be necessary to hide there for some time, I reasoned.

It was to be like this throughout the war. Whatever craft I needed to know to keep us alive, I practiced. A mason, a businessman, a black marketeer, a philosopher, a psychologist, a gardener, or an architect. I mastered all these occupations. Could any of our persecutors have accomplished this? I doubt it.

The German police demanded that the *Judenrat* provide increasingly large sums of money and more workers. Those who could not pay were carted off to slave labor. We could not pay the stipulated sum, because I barely had enough to pay the Germans for the privilege of keeping my business open and living in my own house, so I stayed in the attic nearly all the time. The gold remained untouched. We would need that for the future.

Between October 1939 and January 1940, the Germans issued a series of anti-Jewish decrees. Every Jew over the age of thirteen, male and female, had to wear a four-inch-wide arm band with a blue Star of David on a white background on his or her right arm. Any Jew neglecting the arm band could be executed immediately. The decree depressed many of us greatly. Many young Jews had dressed in the latest fashions and passed as non-Jews, circulating freely and avoiding the labor draft. If they did this now, they risked execution. It was also degrading. Many Poles used the easy identification to ridicule Jews wearing the arm bands.

We thought of escaping to Russian-occupied territory. Just as Stalin and Hitler agreed, the Soviets had invaded on September 17, 1939, shortly after the Germans. The Bug River, about thirty-five miles east of Wegrow, divided the occupied territories, with the Red Army only controlling the extreme eastern portion of Poland. During 1940 and 1941 many younger Jews left everything behind and escaped to the Soviet side. Often, Red Army officers held them prisoner for several days, suspecting that they were German spies, but eventually all were released. Hundreds escaped, only to be captured in 1941 when Hitler turned on Stalin and attacked, overrunning all of Poland and driving deep into the Soviet Union. My mother could not make the arduous trip across the Bug River, which would have required swimming in the dark across narrow creeks and paddling a small boat across rivers, so we decided to stay in our house.

Then another decree was issued. No Jew could buy food in stores. The Germans would distribute rations. A week's rations for one person consisted of one pound of meat, a half pound of sugar, a half pound of butter, and so on. What they distributed could have been eaten at one meal, but it had to last a week. We could not afford to buy on the open market, even if we had been permitted.

Hunger became rampant. People wandered the streets begging for a piece of bread or a potato. When we sat down to eat dinner, people knocked on the door and even the windows, pleading for scraps. If we took pity and opened the door, ten or fifteen people would rush the door and prevent us from closing it. Occasionally, we invited close neighbors to eat with us. Whatever we had, we shared.

More decrees were put forth. Jews must remain in their homes after 6:00 P.M. during the longer days of summer and after 4:00 P.M. during the winter. Curfews lasted until dawn. Every apartment house had a central entrance, and the door had to be locked from the inside at the curfew hour. No non-Jewish doctor or dentist could treat Jews. By this time, the Jewish doctors either had left or had been sent away. If a Jew became ill, Jewish doctors in Warsaw had to be consulted.

We struggled through until spring 1940, when I needed to travel to Warsaw for more merchandise. I obtained permits and hopped aboard the open-bed truck on which Jews had to travel. In Warsaw I saw Poles digging large trenches in the middle of the city. None of the Jews could tell me the purpose of the trenches, but apprehension flowed everywhere. Later, I learned the trenches would provide a base for a huge, brick wall to be erected around the ghetto. The Jews would be sealed in.

The ghetto had deteriorated badly. Ragged, filthy people wandered about in torn, grimy clothes. Many looked like walking skeletons, their ribs protruding grotesquely. The stomachs of the children were distended with malnutrition. Typhus spread and many died. Their bodies lay unattended in the streets because there were too many dead for the burial crews to handle. I bought some merchandise to be shipped home and quickly left the city. I was quite disturbed.

Within a few months, we received word that the ghetto wall had been constructed. New waves of fear enveloped us. Young men and women escaped in increasingly larger numbers to the Soviet side.

Lengthy German army convoys passed through Wegrow. Trucks, tightly covered to conceal their contents, rumbled over the stone streets day and night without pause. The Germans, after a long hesitation over the 1939–40 winter, resumed their conquest of Europe. They rolled into Norway, Belgium, the Netherlands, and France where, to the surprise and horror of the world, the French capitulated quickly. Only the British remained opposed to Hitler in Europe. The Luftwaffe pounded London nightly.

On Yom Kippur day, October 2, 1940, the Warsaw Ghetto was officially established and closed up. All Jews traveling to Warsaw needed special German certificates to visit doctors or dentists or to buy merchandise. I had applied for such a permit, and in October I again traveled to Warsaw to buy clothing. Wearing my arm band, I jumped off the truck and approached the entrance to the ghetto. Two SS men wearing helmets were standing at the guardhouse, armed with machine guns and carrying grenades in their pockets. I trembled at the sight of the German special unit soldiers. They were specially trained to kill Jews.

I flashed my permit and entered the ghetto unhindered. I looked at the wall surrounding the ghetto and my knees felt weak. I had never seen anything like it in my life. It was brick, ten feet tall and one foot thick, with shattered glass cemented to the top.

I had a long way to go on foot. I looked for some kind of transportation, remembering that before the war there had been trolley cars and wagons in Warsaw for public travel. Now there was nothing. I saw an occasional homemade rickshaw fashioned from wood and a bicycle. These were pulled by Jews trying to earn a few zlotys, but I didn't pay much attention. Jews with emaciated bodies, torn clothing, and tattered shoes begged passersby for some coins to buy bread. The bombed-out houses stood like cemetery monuments. The Jews were the living dead.

I made contact with my new acquaintances and business associates. The Christians had all moved to other parts of the city. Jews could not leave. Only a few places were designated as checkpoints; they were guarded day and night by armed soldiers. Food became scarce and people starved, because rations were insufficient. Before construction of the wall, Polish farmers would come to sell their produce in exchange for clothing and other commodities. The wall ended that. At the same time, the Jewish population in the ghetto continued to swell as more Jews were transferred from other towns and villages.

After spending a few days in the ghetto, I felt that this was the end of Warsaw Jewry, and it was clear that the same fate would befall all Polish Jews. However, those in the Warsaw ghetto kept telling me that the Germans would soon be defeated and Hitler and his henchmen would be destroyed. They still hoped that God would help them and that they would witness the destruction of the Nazis. They were not ready to surrender their spirit to the enemy.

What I saw in the ghetto left me very depressed. Everywhere there was hunger, poverty, and typhus. In Wegrow there was no ghetto, but all the Jews had been concentrated in one area. Only in a very few cases did Jews live together with Christians. In Wegrow, too, the situation for Jews was worsening, as the German police were demanding more and more from the Jewish population.

Soon after I returned home, the police came for me to send me on a labor detail. Not finding me at home, they demanded to know from my mother and my sister where I had gone. The women said they did not know. They took Menucha to the office of the Jewish police and told her they would keep her there until I turned myself in. If I did not appear, they threatened that they would send her to forced labor instead of me. My sister was a spirited woman. She was frail-looking and less than five feet tall, but she stood up to the police and was not intimidated. They kept her for twelve hours and then released her.

Menucha realized that they were most likely bluffing since such a small woman could not be of much help in a labor camp. Nor did she fear sexual assault. When the Nazis defeated Poland they issued a decree that Germans were not to have any sexual relations, including rape, with Jewish women. If a German disobeyed this command, he would be killed. We assumed that the reason for this was that Hitler was afraid of polluting Aryan genes by Germans intermingling with Jews. Jewish women may have been assaulted by Germans in other places, but it did not happen in Wegrow. We felt reasonably certain the Germans would obey this decree.

A few days later, when it seemed to be quiet in the street, I went out to pay taxes. As I walked along the street, a German soldier grabbed me by the scruff of the neck and ordered me to follow him to the forced labor group. I told him I was on my way to pay my taxes and that he should let me go. He began shouting at me, so I remained quiet and went with him. With his gun he pushed me off the sidewalk and told me to walk in the street. I became very angry and turned to glare at him. If I had had a gun at that instant, I would not have hesitated to kill him. He kept kicking at my Achilles tendon with his spiked boots until we arrived at the courtyard where the office of the labor authority was located.

Next to the office was an outhouse. He ordered me to remove the feces from the outhouse. He did not provide me with any tools, and I gagged at the thought. Luckily the man whose job it was to do that work was standing nearby. He was a Jew who knew me well. When he saw my predicament he told the German that he would put me to work on the project. The German left. The man told me to stand aside until dusk. I did, and after dark I went home without doing the work. I heard no more about it.

Chapter 3

Survival and Death

I

One thing that made life more tolerable for me was my girlfriend, Rachel Mandelbaum. Before the war I used to go for walks with her and two of her girlfriends. We went to movies and attended meetings of Jabotinski's Zionist Revisionist organization. Rachel and I were attracted to each other. When the war broke out, it was more difficult to walk together in public, because I had to avoid work details. Zionist group meetings were banned, so Rachel came to our house. She walked the streets freely because she had a pass from the German authorities. She designed hats and visited the wives of German soldiers in the evenings to take their special orders. We spent hours together, walking in the enclosed yard, talking, and embracing. We tried to see each other every night. Some sanity crept into an insane world.

Once she became ill, and with no telephones, I had no way of finding out why she did not arrive at the usual time. I became concerned and imagined all sorts of disasters. What would I do without Rachel? What reason would I have to bear this terrible existence? I would not want to go on. Rachel kept me alive, and I knew that some day we would marry and the world would be right again. Her sister finally arrived with Rachel's pass to tell me what had happened, and I thanked God she was safe.

Rachel was intelligent, and we communicated well. Often she would know what I was going to say before I said it. We had the private communication that exists between two young people in love. She would sometimes tell me that if something bad happened to me, she would take her own life. We loved each other dearly. When she could not come to see me, I missed her terribly. I felt as if she were part of me. She was a warm, lovable person who could engage almost anyone in conversation.

Attractive but not gorgeous, she dressed in the latest styles and could converse with both Christian and Jewish women about fashions or any number of other topics. She was slim with a narrow face and attractive features except for a larger than usual nose, which was typical of Eastern European Jews. She numbered many Christians among her friends, as well as Jews.

Rachel. Rachel. I thought of her, and the days passed more easily. The Germans had taken away almost everything, but what Rachel and I had, they could not take away. When I had spare moments, I thought of what Rachel and I could talk about at our next meeting. I would invent ways to buoy her spirits and get our minds off the world around us. Her touch would make me feel like a man, and I knew I could face almost anyone or anything. Her embrace replenished my spirits, and her kiss healed my anguish. Marriage was unthinkable in these times. But some day. Some day. Some day.

It was because of Rachel's connections that I was able to avoid the labor force. Her friend Rochma Rajzman worked as secretary to the president of the *Judenrat*. She knew when the orders would be given to take certain young men for forced labor. Rochma promised to tell Rachel when her brothers would be taken by the Jewish police, and Rachel also convinced her to tell her when they would be coming for me. When I learned of such an order, I slept in the attic hiding place. This occurred many times. The police could not find me.

II

The time had come for us all to take a hard look at how the Bielawskis were going to avoid extermination. The family gathered in the kitchen and we weighed every possible option. Jews continued to escape to the Soviet side as conditions worsened, and we wondered again if we should not do the same. My mother would have difficulty making such a journey, but Yitzchak and I could sneak over to the Soviet side and see whether a permanent move was feasible.

We had heard that Polish thugs attacked Jews on the road at night and took their belongings. The victims could not yell or protest for fear of being discovered by the Germans and shot, so we had to plan the journey with great care to avoid being seen.

Polish currency had no exchange value on the other side; the Soviets did not accept it. We each took six pieces of leather, about two feet square. Because the war had disrupted the leather manufacturing industry, the raw material was scarce and expensive. A person could live a week from the sale of one piece of leather. We planned to stay for about one week. If we could find somewhere to live and work, we would return and take the entire family.

On a crisp autumn day in 1940, Yitzchak and I prepared to cross the Bug River. We hired a gentile to hide us in his horse-drawn wagon as he traveled east to Sokolow at night. From there we paid another man to take us further the next night. A light rain fell as the second driver dropped us off two miles from the river. He told us to travel in a straight line, and when we came to the bank, another man would ferry us across the river in his small boat. As we walked, the rainfall intensified, soaking us. At the side of the river stood a tall, robust man. He told us he wanted 100 zlotys ($35) in advance. We paid the outrageous sum, because we had no choice. This man stood by the river in the middle of the night so that he could extort money from hapless Jews, who he knew would be trying to escape. For him, money had never flowed so freely.

He pointed to a canoe and told us to sit still and hold on tight, because the canoe could easily capsize. I realized he might try to drown us in the river. We took our seats and he rowed.

We reached the east bank without incident and wandered in the dark aimlessly trying to find our way. Within five minutes, two soldiers with rifles stood before us and ordered us to raise our hands.

"Why are you here in the middle of the night?" one barked.

"We are escaping from the Germans," I answered.

"You're lying. You're smugglers and should be shot," he retorted.

They led us to a concrete building and forced us inside, where hundreds of people sat on a cement floor in a large, barren room. They were all Jews—men, women, and children. We joined them on the cold floor. There was no place even to lay my head. There was only enough room to sit side by side. Exhausted, we sat this way until we dozed.

In the morning, Soviet soldiers came in and ordered everyone to stand, if he wanted to eat. Everyone got up. Two Red Army soldiers at the doorway threw in pieces of bread, as if they were feeding animals at a zoo. Everyone stretched out his hands. The longer the arm, the greater the chance of getting some. Yitzchak and I caught one piece, which we shared.

The bread was black and not fully baked. It looked like a mixture of clay and dust, and was unsalted and dry, and difficult to swallow. I chewed until my jaws would not work anymore. I did not know how long we would have to sit there or when we would be fed again so I choked the bread down. I asked some of the others how long they had been in the place, and most told me two or three days. They said that they had been taken to the interrogation section for questioning. With luck one could be freed right away, but some had been detained for weeks.

We stood near the window. There were only two eighteen-inch by twenty-four-inch barred windows in the whole building, which was about forty by seventy feet. The room in which we were kept was about forty feet square. A second smaller room housed the offices of the Soviet jail keepers and was divided from our room by a thick, cement brick wall with a door. Our room had no furniture, just a cement floor and cement-block walls. The toilet was outside. Each time a person had to use it, he had to pound on the wall and get one of the jailers to take him outside.

Through a window, we watched soldiers passing. Repeatedly, we knocked at the window and asked about our release. Soldiers passed, but did not stop. Finally, one did and I told him that we were wet, cold, and hungry. A half hour later, he returned and took us to the office, where he questioned us.

"Where are you from and why have you come here?"

"We are Jews from the German side. They are starving and beating Jews daily. We cannot live there anymore, so we crossed the border to find a better life."

"Did you bring anything with you?"

"We are shoemakers and managed to keep pieces of leather from the Germans." We showed him the leather.

"You are smugglers! We should shoot you!"

"We are not. We are not. We had to hide the leather to keep from being robbed."

He left us alone and returned a minute later. "Take your leather and leave." We did not argue.

Outside, we found out that we had been in a fifty-year-old building in the country about three miles from Siemiatycze, a city of 5,000 that once belonged to Poland but was now a part of the Soviet Union due to the Hitler-Stalin pact. The building had apparently been converted from a large farm storage shed.

We walked to Siemiatycze, where we saw much Soviet military equipment and large crowds in the streets. A tour of the city brought us to a bustling marketplace, a *tolchok*, where everything could be bought and sold. After buying some food, we asked where we could spend the night. A few of the marketers showed us a house where the owner rented space for sleeping. They warned us that the proprietor insisted on no less than two people in one bed. We rented a bed, paying in advance. Each room contained rude bunks, nailed loosely together. Pillows were actually sacks stuffed with straw and mattresses were loose straw over boards.

After supper, we walked the streets, asked around, and learned that most of the people cramming the market were Jews escaping the Germans. Everyone sought work, but no jobs existed. We returned to our rented room, exhausted and discouraged. Our bed was so narrow that we had to sleep on our sides. Sleep came quickly, but we awakened three hours later with our sides hurting. After exchanging places, we fell back asleep on the opposite sides.

The next morning we went to the marketplace and sold some leather to get money for food and lodging.

"Why is it so crowded here?" I asked a passer-by. "Why don't Jews migrate further into the Soviet Union?"

"The Russians are so afraid of spies that they do not allow Jews to go further, so Jews keep jamming into the border area," he answered.

Stalin and Hitler may have signed a pact, but the Soviets did not trust the Germans. Apparently, the Soviets had no more interest in helping Jews than did the Poles. There was no way to earn a living. As long as Jews had some money, the Soviets allowed them to stay, but when the money ran out, the refugees could expect no help. As it was, sanitation was poor and the food was almost inedible. Without money, not even that food could be had. If anyone complained he was told, "Go back where you came from!"

We entered a restaurant looking for some warm food, which we had not had for four days, and waited half an hour for a table. A Jewish waiter came over and took our order. He asked us to pay in advance. Another half hour passed before he served us watery soup with a few noodles floating in it.

As we finished eating, the waiter approached our table. Breathing heavily and wheezing, he shouted, "Get up and leave! We have more customers who need this table!" He leaned on our table and coughed violently, spitting up clumps of green phlegm onto the floor beside our table. I gagged, nearly losing the "hot meal" I had just eaten. We needed no further encouragement to leave.

Over the next four days we checked out the town thoroughly. No baths. Little food. No jobs. Hardly a place to sleep. Could we bring the entire family here? We would die from cold, hunger, or disease. As bad as it was in Wegrow, it was still more intolerable there.

Out of money as well as enthusiasm, we started home. Leaving was much easier than entering. In fact, the Russians were only too eager to help us on our way. In Wegrow, we related our experiences to a disappointed family, who had counted on escaping the Germans. If only someone somewhere could have provided a home for Jews. We were trapped in a grisly web from which there was no escape.

III

A few days later, when I cautiously ventured outside, a German appeared from a side street, grabbed me, and put me on a truck. Along with several other Jewish men, I stood in the open truck as it rumbled over five miles of unpaved road to the small village of Live near the Liwiec River on the way to Warsaw. A makeshift bridge, constructed with my lumber, spanned the river. It had replaced the regular structure which was destroyed in the early days of the war. Now, the Germans wanted to build a more permanent bridge again.

As I got off the truck, I saw about forty or fifty Jews standing in water up to their hips digging post holes. That, it seemed, would be how I would spend the day. But the gentile carpenters working on the wooden bridge superstructure saw me and told the German supervisor that they wanted me to work with them because I was a skilled carpenter. They had done business with me and knew me well. I started the carpentry work, thankful that I would not have to stand in the chilly water all day.

A half hour later, a German officer dressed in green with a large feather in his hat approached. Puffing on his pipe, he inquired, "Who here can speak German?" No one answered.

Finally, I said in German, "I can."

"Come over here," he said, and I complied. "Get a horse and wagon and go to town to buy tobacco for my pipe. Here is the address." He handed me a sheet of paper and wrote below the address the name of the brand that he wanted. Then he scribbled a message for the store-keeper, asking him to give me the tobacco without money, assuring the storekeeper that the army would pay later. He signed the note. "Return quickly and I will assign you to light work for the rest of the day," he commanded.

I took the horse and wagon to town, where I purchased the tobacco, and stopped at home to tell my family what had happened. After a quick lunch, I returned to Live and gave the officer his tobacco.

"Thank you, young man," he said. "Now take the horse and wagon to pick up some logs over in the forest three kilometers that way. Choose some other workers for loading and unloading the wagon."

I chose several men who seemed exhausted and told them not to hurry. At night they freed all of us, and we returned home. Once again, I managed to survive a work detail. How long would my luck last?

The next day some SS men ordered the *Judenrat* to choose workers for assignment to Treblinka. The Jews returned later in the week, saying that they had chopped down trees and laid trestles for a railroad track. Hundreds of workers were building something, but no one knew what. Each day, the Germans demanded more workers for the death camp. Treblinka and Auschwitz, also in Poland, were two of the most infamous of the Nazi concentration camps. This was the beginning of plans to systematically exterminate the Jews of Poland.

About a week later, the Germans hung a loudspeaker on a post in the market square and told the townspeople that everyone must listen to a speech from Adolf Hitler. The German leader told his countrymen how strong they were. Then he shouted in a powerful voice, saying that all Jews in Europe were going to be destroyed. If one Jew remained after the war, he personally would salute him, Hitler boasted.

The Jews lowered their heads in grief. Could this be? The Nazis told lies as a matter of course. They lied about everything to fool the world and to conceal their real goals. How could anyone believe anything Hitler said? No one would simply annihilate an entire race of people for no good reason! This was the twentieth century, not the Middle Ages. The Jews believed that they would survive Hitler as Jews had always survived for thousands of years. God always helped, and they believed this would be the case now.

I traveled to Warsaw for supplies, so that we could stay in business. There, the ghetto had become a desolate hellhole. The only means of transportation was a two-passenger bicycle-wheel ricksha, pedaled from behind by a Jew. I saw many of these. There was not enough food for horses. The thought of having a human being pedal me along in a ricksha revolted me, so I waited a while in vain for another mode of transportation. Eventually, I relented and signaled a ricksha.

"I feel badly about having you pull me along," I told the driver.

"Can you better stand the thought of my wife and children dying of hunger? Which is worse?" he answered.

I could not believe how terrible the people looked. Along the walls of bombed-out buildings sat skeleton-like creatures begging for food. I was dumbfounded. Scavengers combed through garbage. Once, I watched some ragged people hungrily shove rotting potato peels into their mouths. To stay alive, men became animals.

Hitler was indeed carrying out his threat to destroy the Jews. Merchants confirmed that things were going from bad to worse, but said that many Jews would survive, though others would die of starvation, exposure, and disease. The Poles needed the Jews from whom they obtained finished goods, the merchants said. Poles smuggled in the rough skins, the Jews produced the finished leather. In exchange for the leather goods and other crafted products, Poles smuggled in food. It was a matter of economics, I was told. The Poles could not afford to lose the Jews.

The Jews continued to live by their wits. On Ulica Wolnosci (Freedom Street), one side was in the ghetto and the other was outside the wall. Germans bricked up all the doors and windows on the Jewish side. The Poles agreed that in exchange for finished goods, they would supply milk for the Jewish children. They poured milk into the roof gutters on their side, and the Jews caught the milk on the other side in pails at the bottom of the drains.

My heart was full of pain, and I could not stand to see such suffering.

The world was deaf and did not hear the cries. Yet, these starving, ragged creatures fought on. Few committed suicide. They waited and hoped for help from anywhere. They prayed for world pity, but in particular they hoped that the United States would come to their rescue. They were certain that if the Americans only knew what was happening, they would not allow it to continue. They prayed to the United States as if to God.

When I returned home, I heard from some farmers from the Treblinka area that the Germans were building barracks and houses there. The entire place was surrounded with electrified barbed wire. It was all very secret.

The flow of trucks, artillery, tanks, and other military hardware through Wegrow in the direction of the Soviet Union suddenly increased. No one understood why so much military hardware was being transported, but it soon became clear. Hitler turned on Stalin in June 1941 and attacked the Soviet Union.

Our living conditions continued to worsen. Unemployment increased and poverty became more widespread. As people became hungrier and weaker, typhus spread to an epidemic. The community had no Jewish doctors now and little medicine for Jews. The *Judenrat* could not meet the Germans' demands for money, so the Nazis threatened to ship the entire Jewish community of Wegrow to Warsaw. Beatings and labor roundups became routine.

I slept regularly in the attic hiding place, and I remained in hiding around the clock, eluding the Jewish police successfully for months.

The Germans enjoyed themselves, partying, dancing, and drinking within our earshot. Polish girls joined in the festivities. The Polish gentiles seemed quite at ease fraternizing with their conquerors. Collaborating with the Germans did not seem to bother them in the least. Seeing all this only served to increase our suffering. I would have thought that the Poles would hate the Germans and do everything they could to drive these murderers from their homeland, but they seemed more interested in making the most of the moment. No gentile ever came to us and asked us if he could help us, or if we needed anything. No one lifted a finger to ease our plight in any way.

The beginning of 1941 brought no relief. If a Pole desired the business of a Jew, he would simply tell the housing authority and they would evict the Jewish owner. This occurred frequently. The only way to keep a business was with bribes.

Poles would come into Jewish businesses to examine merchandise. If they found empty shelves, they reported this to the Germans, who then confiscated the store. It was vital to keep shelves well stocked.

Again I traveled to Warsaw and as I entered the ghetto I saw wagons sagging with the weight of dead bodies. Arms and legs protruded beneath sheets of newspaper. I became numb. Dead bodies were being stacked and transported like so much firewood. The driver said that hundreds were dying of hunger and typhus. The burial society could not keep up with their tasks, and corpses lay in the streets or on sidewalks for several days. There was not enough linen to make burial shrouds for proper Jewish burials. They were buried in paper.

I was dazed. Time seemed to stand still. When the driver stopped at my destination, I could not move. He waited until I had regained my senses. I don't know how long that was.

I stayed indoors all day, so I would not have to look at such suffering. The next morning, I again went out and saw the skeleton-like figures propped against the walls, attempting to play violins, waiting for pennies to be dropped. I saw people with faces as large as pumpkins, swollen from hunger. They could no longer walk. Passers-by hurried on quickly. I soon found out why. While I was walking slowly, I was surrounded by poor people begging for coins. As soon as I gave out some money, I was completely inundated and barely escaped from the mob. When I went looking for my old sellers, I found that many had died in the epidemic or moved. Finally, I found alternate sellers and made my purchases.

Then, as I started toward the gate to the ghetto, I reached into my pocket for my papers. They were gone! I didn't know how or where, but I had lost my travel permit. I could not escape the ghetto. This pitiful den of pestilence and starvation would be my burial chamber. I would die in the Warsaw ghetto, one of hundreds of thousands of nameless, faceless Jews. My mother, sister, and brothers would never know what had become of me. Rachel and I would never see each other again.

Then I drew in my breath and the panic ended. I asked how I might obtain an exit permit and obtained an address, that, as it turned out, belonged to an old acquaintance of mine from the town of Sokolow. He told me that he could help me, but that it would cost me more than 300 zlotys. I agreed. He took me to a place where trucks from the gas and electric company stood. Metal barrels sat in the beds of the trucks.

The man said, "The gas and electric companies have permission to go in and out of the ghetto as needed to make repairs. I have a 'business' arrangement with the truck driver. Hide in one of the metal barrels and remain quiet, because the Germans will stop the truck for inspection of documents and of the truck's contents."

I crawled into an empty barrel, my heart pounding. The truck pulled away and stopped at the guard station. The German asked about the supplies on the truck, and the driver told him the barrels were empty. The guard walked along the side of the truck inspecting the truck bed. I could hear his slow, deliberate footsteps approaching. I held my breath. If he found me there, I would be finished. He walked slowly, back and forth. I could only hear the sound of footsteps. I could count the steps.

He paused. He walked. He paused. Satisfied, he ordered the driver to pass.

The truck driver transported me to a freight truck going to Wegrow, carrying both passengers and goods. I reached home without further incident, but my knees were still weak.

IV

A few days later I developed a high fever and my mother summoned the medic, Nathan Weintraub. He examined me and told me I had typhus. "Stay in bed until the fever abates. I will leave some medicine." To my mother he said, "Call if his condition does not improve."

The next day my fever rose, but Weintraub was busy with other patients. As I lay in bed delirious, a knock came at the door. Thinking it was Weintraub, my mother answered, and in came a German officer.

"Where are the men of the house?" he demanded.

"There are no men in the house," my mother said. He opened the door to the bedroom and saw me. He turned to my mother and slapped her with his open palm, knocking her to the floor.

"Liar!" he screamed. He strode over to me and slapped me until I passed out. Then he left when he saw that I could do no work.

For a long time I remained unconscious, and when I awakened, the fever kept me delirious. My family purchased ice, so that I could keep an ice pack on my forehead. Weintraub found that my temperature was extremely high, even with ice. He gave me a shot in my hip and my leg swelled painfully, but still the fever did not abate.

"That is all I can do. Watch him carefully tonight. If he survives the night, he will recover," Weintraub told my mother.

The whole family sat that night in a silent vigil, checking on me periodically, changing the ice packs, and taking my pulse. Somehow in my delirium, I still realized my condition was grave, but it didn't bother me. Life had become so unpleasant that I did not really care if I lived or died. I thought about the Warsaw Ghetto. I felt that I would rather die then and there, than wait to die a slow death of hunger and be thrown into an unmarked grave. At least here I would be with my family and be assured of a decent burial. Death seemed to be more bearable than life. But once again I lived.

In the morning the medic came to check on me. As soon as he saw me, he put his palm to my forehead and announced that I had recovered. The family celebrated. I stayed in bed for another week gradually regaining my health. Not many Jews survived a bout of typhus in Poland in 1941, but for whatever reason, I continued to live.

Still, I had to return to hiding. Jewish workers now traveled daily to Treblinka for construction work, as well as to Mord, where they drained marshy fields. I avoided work details until, once again, on April 20, 1941, I happened to be in the house when two German soldiers came to the door. They took me to the marketplace. There, I saw about a hundred Jews from all walks of life lined up in rows of four each. We marched to the local sports arena, where the Germans had taken over a locker room and storage building. They had converted the building to an Army headquarters. We saw wagons, horses, freight trucks, and German officers awaiting us. Each officer chose workers for a specific task. One wanted twenty workers for unloading grain twenty-four miles outside town. Others wanted workers for feeding horses, cleaning up after them, and brushing their coats.

An officer approached the waiting workers and asked, "Who can buy butter?"

When no one responded, I stepped forward. He took me past a guardhouse into the building and to his office, where I was greeted by a large portrait of Hitler hanging on the wall. Hitler's arm was outstretched in the Nazi salute. The picture reminded me of where I was and who I was. I was frightened and thought I was going to be shot on the spot. He took me over to a desk and told the official there that I was a Jew who could buy butter for them.

"What is the price for butter?" he asked.

I knew that butter could only be bought on the black market at five zlotys per kilo (eighty cents a pound), but I said I did not know.

"It costs five zlotys per kilo," he said.

"That may be so."

"I need five kilos because it is Hitler's birtday. We need to bake cakes in preparation for a great celebration." He gave me twenty-five zlotys. "I'll go with you and stand off in the distance, while you buy the butter."

"If you go with me, I will be unable to buy the butter, because no one would complete a black market sale with a German officer standing nearby." Since he had to have the butter, he had no choice but to let me make the purchase alone, so he agreed. "What would prevent another German soldier from diverting me to another forced labor battalion and taking the money from me? Give me a certificate saying that I work exclusively for you and I can show it to anyone who might try to interfere."

He went over to the desk officer to explain, and then I said in German that the certificate should read: "Regularly employed by the German armed forces." He wrote it up and stamped it with the official German seal. He gave it to me and ordered, "Return promptly and I will send you back home for the day." The guards were ordered to allow me to enter when I returned.

I went home and told my family what had happened, ate, and then went to see a woman acquaintance who handled dairy products. She agreed to lower the price to four and a half zlotys per kilo, so I kept some money.

I took my time going back to the military station because I wanted them to forget about the certificate. At the station, the officer took me inside, opened the package, and tasted some of the butter on his finger. He was so pleased that he took me into the next room and offered me a cigar from the desk.

"Thanks, but I don't smoke," I said.

"Oh, but you must take one," he said amiably. "You are a good Jew. Have a cigar."

I took it. Amazing. This man represented an occupation army bent upon total annihilation of my people and here he was offering me a cigar as if we were old chums. The world had gone crazy!

"Do you know someone who could make a good pair of officer's boots for me?" he inquired.

"I'll ask around," I answered.

"Fine," he said. "Now you go on home and come back tomorrow and let me know if you have found a good shoemaker." He forgot about the certificate, which I kept, figuring that it would come in handy someday. I had also earned two and a half zlotys on the butter deal. I told my family about the certificate and warned them not to tell anyone else about it.

I decided not to return the next day. The officer came to the *Judenrat* and demanded to know why I had not come back with the certificate. He told them to find me and the pass. My name was not on their work list, so they could not trace the pass to me. They sent Jewish policemen to find it, and one asked me if I knew who had bought butter for the Germans. With the pass in my pocket, I told him I knew nothing.

Dodging the Jewish police, the German soldiers, and the Polish civilians became increasingly difficult, and a week later on a Sunday afternoon a German soldier carrying a machine gun broke in and grabbed me by the collar.

"I work for the German Army," I said producing the pass.

"What are you doing home instead of working?"

"It is Sunday. The Army gave me the day off."

He let me go and left. Menucha went outside and watched as the Germans sent about fifty people away for labor.

Weeks later, I needed to go outside for an errand and once again a soldier grabbed me. I had to go with him. I dared not produce the certificate in public, fearing that someone would realize that I was the one who had not returned the pass to the Germans. I would certainly have been handed over to the army and shot.

An officer asked for a volunteer for gardening. I stepped forward. He wanted a garden around his quarters, and I began the work. After two hours, he saw that the lines of stones around the garden were straight and the work neat. Pleased, he brought me some food. I thanked him but said I wasn't hungry. He again came out at the end of the day and expressed satisfaction. He complimented me and my two helpers, although we had not worked too hard or too fast. He said he would send us home, but told me to return the next day to finish up. I did not return and again the *Judenrat* searched for the missing gardener, so I was afraid to go out even more than usual for fear of being recognized.

V

Again, I needed to travel to Warsaw for merchandise. I was not eager to go, but without the business we would not be able to continue living in the house, so I applied for a permit to replace the one I had lost. Travel regulations had now tightened and the Germans told me to come back in several weeks.

I could not wait that long, so I took a gamble and used the old certificate the German officer had given me. I told the guards at the ghetto that I needed medical attention for a stomach problem, and they let me enter.

The beggars were gone. Mounds lay on the pavement, covered with paper. Bricks weighted the paper down and prevented it from blowing away. A ricksha driver explained that the beggars had finally died of starvation and exposure, and the corpses lay in the street for as much as two or three days awaiting burial. Large pits served as mass burial sites. Not enough paper existed to wrap each body separately.

I couldn't believe what was happening as I walked through the ghetto. Every hundred feet or so I passed another lifeless mound. Occasionally, a gust of wind would lift the paper and reveal the corpse underneath. In one place the wind uncovered the body of a young girl, her face pretty and her hair long and blonde. She must have been twelve or thirteen years old. She seemed to be sleeping peacefully, and I couldn't believe she was dead. After I continued a few paces, I returned to see if she were really dead. To this day the vision of that young girl, her hair finely combed and her face so peaceful, pursues me. I cannot remove the image from my mind. The Nazi pig bastards killed everyone, including innocent children. Who appointed them executioners of everything living? Who decided that a twelve-year-old child should be starved to death and her precious, little body left to die anonymously on the street?

I was truly sorry this time that I had come to Warsaw. I cannot possibly describe the suffering. Incredibly, Jews died of starvation, and just on the other side of the wall people lived in luxury, eating, drinking, and partying. They bought valuable Jewish possessions for a crust of bread, the valuables of Jews whose families had lived as Polish citizens for hundreds of years.

How could this be justified or explained? Although I did not know it then, in Norway, Holland, Belgium, Finland, and many other places in Europe, large segments of the population risked their lives daily to protect Jews from the Nazis. But not in Poland. In Poland, hardly anyone cared to save even one Jewish life. We had lived next door to each other for generations and yet we did not know one another.

How could anyone find logic in 1941 Poland? The starving person does not understand why his life must end, why he must go to the grave prematurely. He has done nothing to deserve this. He knows that his oppressors, those responsible for his death, are on the other side of this wall. Yet the pain of hunger is not as great as the scorn and ridicule and humiliation. The inhuman creatures on the other side of the wall seem to be saying by their actions, "You Jews are so clever. Yet it will not help you. You will die anyway." He demands to know of God why this is happening to him. Are we not Your chosen people? Why don't You keep your promises to us? Do You think You can exchange us for a better people? Thoughts and questions race through the mind, but there are no answers.

On their side the Christians ate and drank, and on our side we starved. They could not say they did not know what was going on. They saw it daily with their own eyes. They could hear the cries from across the wall.

In one place, on Zelazna Street, the Christian section was situated between two Jewish sections. The Jews could travel from one side to the other by crossing an iron bridge that spanned the Polish section. The Poles could see how the Jews looked as they walked across or stood on the bridge. The Jewish children were thin and emaciated, begging for bread. "Help us," they cried. "Our parents are dead. Take pity on us." But the Polish women, who had children of their own, looked on unmoved. The Jewish children starved.

No pity. No remorse. Poland was an agricultural country with a surplus of food. Before the war, food was a major export, and even now, the Germans did not drain the supply of meat and vegetables too greatly. No, it was not the war that was killing these people. It was what was in the hearts of their oppressors and their countrymen.

I remained in the ghetto only two days. This would be my last trip to Warsaw during the war. Before leaving I met Rachel, through a prior arrangement. She had also come to the ghetto to buy material for her hats. She wanted to return home with me when my work was done.

As we passed the German guard, we asked a Polish carriage driver to take us to the trucks bound for Wegrow. A few blocks down the road, a seventeen-year-old Polish boy riding a bicycle stopped the carriage. "Are you wearing your Jewish arm bands?" he demanded. We said we were. Then he said. "Because you are Jews, you are not allowed in the Polish areas. Either you give me a hundred zlotys ($35) or I will take you back to the German guard!"

I knew that if I gave this scoundrel the money, others would do the same. I produced my German army pass and showed him the seal and the swastika. I turned to the driver and said, "You are my witness that he does not recognize the authority of the German seal. Take us all back to the guard and we will tell him so!"

Frightened, the driver started to turn the carriage, but the Polish boy quickly mounted his bicycle and rode off. My bold facade had saved us, but inwardly both Rachel and I quaked. We returned home without further incident.

Soon we began hearing horrible stories from the farmers in the Treblinka area. They saw railroad cars packed with Jewish men, women, and children heading to the camp. Many jumped from the train and died. The Germans shot others who were not killed in the jump. Daily, the screaming continued as the trains entered Treblinka, but shortly after the trains entered, all was silent, and the trains came back out empty. A continuous plume of smoke hung above Treblinka, the farmers said, and they smelled the stench of burning flesh.

The Germans had chosen wholesale murder. There could no longer be any denial of the truth or of what the future held. We were dumbstruck. Was it actually possible that Hitler was making good on his promise to exterminate European Jewry?

We did not know what to do. Some of my old friends from the rightist Zionist organization, Jabotinsky's Revisionist group, got together to discuss organizing resistance. We elected Zeynwill Szpilman as leader.

But what could we do? The Germans possessed machine guns, tanks, and grenades. We had nothing, not even a single gun. Many Poles, especially farmers in isolated farmhouses, had illegally obtained guns and rifles to defend themselves. These had been smuggled out of the police force or the army. Jews, however, were not farmers. They had found no need for guns in the cities. Jews did not hunt game, because animals killed by a rifle shot do not provide kosher meat. Only an animal slaughtered with one quick stroke of a long-bladed knife is kosher. This God commanded; this way the animal does not suffer. That is the dietary law. Also, the Talmud directs Jews not to hunt for pleasure, because killing animals for such reasons is not according to the precepts of the Torah. So Jews had no need for hunting rifles. Before the war, the Polish government banned ownership of handguns or other non-sporting firearms, so few had other sorts of weapons. I had heard of only one Jew who had a small pistol. When the Germans came for him, he flashed the pistol and they retreated quickly, blowing up the house with hand grenades and killing the man and his family in the house. The Germans always traveled in groups even when just walking down the street, so it was nearly impossible to stalk a soldier, kill him, and grab his weapon. The Germans did not trust the Poles and certainly not the Jews.

We decided to secretly speak to other young Jews who might be willing to join us. We also approached some of the Jews in town who still had some money. We explained that death was now at our doorsteps and that we needed cash to obtain weapons. The odds were overwhelmingly against us, but they realized how desperate the situation was and were willing to help.

Secretly, we met with representatives of the Polish underground, members of the Polish Party Socialists. They were bitter enemies of the Germans, themselves. We told them we wanted to buy guns to fight the Germans. No price was too high. They asked for time to consult their leadership.

Several months went by, and we heard nothing from them. Finally, they replied that they had no weapons available, but that they would do what they could to obtain some. They told us to have patience. We had no patience and no time. Still, we waited. They never furnished us with any weapons.

Meanwhile, the Germans demanded ever more money from the *Judenrat*. They threatened to turn Wegrow into a permanent ghetto and to draft more Jews for labor at Treblinka. The *Judenrat* must have known what was going on at the death camp, because they strived mightily to meet the Germans' demands.

When enough money was not forthcoming, the Jewish police consolidated several families into one house and forced anyone who had any money to pay vast sums. We were threatened with loss of our house and business if we could not come up with cash. We faced the possibility of another family living in our home, but we knew that no change in residence could be effected without the authorization of the housing administration.

I knew the two *Volksdeutsch* officials in charge, the two I had befriended and given shirts, when they first arrived in Wegrow. I went to one of them with a gift and told him that the *Judenrat* had threatened to put another family in our house. He said that no transfers could occur without his permission, and that if the Jewish police came to bring another family, I should call him immediately. He said he would take care of it.

Several days passed. On a Friday morning, six Jewish police arrived with a wagon containing an old table and chairs, a bed and bedding, and several pieces of broken and battered furniture. On top of the heap sat a man, his wife, and his two children, aged seven and ten. I locked the door, and Menucha and my sister-in-law went to tell the housing administrator. We asked the police to wait while we tried to contact the *Judenrat*.

But they did not wait. They began to chop down our door, a solid wood door two-and-a-half inches thick. I could do nothing but sit at the front of the store.

A young woman, my Christian neighbor, ran to tell me what the police were doing to my beautiful door. I told her I had to wait for the housing administrator, but she dragged me over to the police. Quietly, I approached one of the young policemen, who was about eighteen years old, and asked him whether he had ever earned enough to pay for such a door. Suddenly, the commander of the police, Noah Kochman, came over and slapped me in the face. Furious, I struck him in the face with my fist. Blood streamed down his forehead. I had punched him in the front of his police cap, and the screw attaching the metal insignia to his cap had cut the forehead.

He yelled that I was killing him, and the others attacked me one at a time. As each came toward me, I hit him in the face. They could not subdue me! Finally, the commander told his men to bring the Polish police. The Jewish police tried to drag me off, but I grabbed the spokes of a wagon standing in the lumberyard. They pulled so hard, and I held on so firmly, that they dragged the wagon and the horses as well! They gave up.

Soon two Polish policemen came and told me to follow them to the police station nearby. "You know me as a peaceful person. I fought only in self-defense," I said. "Stand back and I will go peacefully." The Polish police told everyone to leave, and we walked to the station.

As soon as I entered, Noah attacked me with his rubber truncheon. I ducked and grabbed it from him, hitting him with his own weapon, all the while yelling so that the Polish police outside would think I was being beaten.

Finally, the Polish police came in and restrained me. "We have to arrest you," one said, "because you attacked the Jewish police. That is against the law."

They took me to the jail about two blocks away and locked me in a cell with twenty other Jewish prisoners. When I told the other prisoners my story, they were quite pleased, because they had all been locked up by the Jewish police for not reporting for labor.

At about nine o'clock in the evening, we heard the outer door open, and in came the Polish commander with the Jewish police chief. They told me to go into the adjoining dark room. I smelled brandy on the Polish commander's breath. It was clear they wanted to beat me, so I climbed the table beneath the cell window and held onto the bars. The Pole came to get me down, but I kicked at him. After a few more unsuccessful tries, he gave up and left.

Two hours later, another policeman came in and told me I could leave. I was afraid to go, thinking they were waiting outside to attack me. He told me Menucha and my sister-in-law would take me home. I said I would leave only if I heard it directly from them. They came in and I left with them.

In the station office waited the president of the *Judenrat*, the Polish commander, Noah Kochman, and several other Jewish policemen. "Striking a policeman is a serious offense. You are liable for a severe punishment," the commander told me. But they had known me and my family for many years, and as he put it, "Sometimes a priest becomes a bandit."

"Because this is your first offense, we will let you go, if you promise to return tomorrow and apologize," he added.

"I have nothing to apologize for," I said. "They came to my house illegally, began chopping down my door, and then began beating me. So I defended myself. They owe me an apology! I would rather return to prison than apologize."

"Go home and we'll decide what to do with you in the morning," I was told. I was sure that the housing administrator had told them to release me. Later, I found out that after he had heard from Menucha, he went to the president of the *Judenrat* and demanded to know by what authority he had sent men to chop down the door of a German-owned house. He told the president that he, himself, could be arrested for carrying out this action without permission from the housing authority. He gave him one hour to have me released and told him that no other families were to be moved into our house, because there was no room.

I knew that the Jewish police would try to get even and seize me for labor at their earliest opportunity. They came looking for me the next day, but I hid.

On June 22, 1941, Hitler shocked the world by attacking the Soviet Union all along the eastern border of German-occupied Poland. The Germans quickly advanced and the beleaguered Red Army, caught unprepared, retreated. Wherever the Germans found Jews along their eastward march, they killed them.

Eight days later an order was issued that all clothing made of fur had to be turned over to the Germans. The pretext for the order was that German soldiers would need warm coats on the eastern front, and the penalty for not obeying it was death. And so Jewish men gave up their coats as did the women.

As we continued to hear reports of Jews being killed at Treblinka, we again agonized over what to do. Several young Jews who had attended Polish high schools and colleges and who did not look particularly Jewish were able to obtain fake passports. They changed their names and moved to larger cities where they tried to live as gentiles. Many were caught and executed.

The Germans boasted that they were doing so well on the Russian front that they would soon be in Moscow. We heard German soldiers yelling, "We see Moscow!" as their army trucks passed through the streets of Wegrow. We knew that the more powerful the Germans became, the longer we could expect the war to last.

As 1942 began, our lives became nearly intolerable. We had lived with extortion, murder, beatings, and forced labor for more than two years, but the worst was yet to come. The commandant of Treblinka demanded more and more Jews for labor. Those who were sent did not return. Jews no longer offered themselves passively for the labor force. They resisted, but still many were forced at gunpoint to go.

Jewish businesses closed at an ever-increasing rate. Our neighbor, Fishel Chudzik, had operated a restaurant in his building for years. Maniek Karbowski, the seventeen-year-old son of a Polish policeman, asked the housing people for half of Chudzik's place. The order went out, and Maniek received half ownership.

Maniek was a thin, long-faced youth with straight blond hair and shifty eyes. He had great ambitions, but never wanted to work for anything. Everything he wanted had to come the easy way. He never looked anyone in the eye. You couldn't trust anything he said. His father, a policeman, was no better—untrustworthy and lazy. Often, he bought on credit, but he never paid his bill. They lived on the other side of the lumberyard, about three blocks away. Soon after the invasion, the Germans caught Maniek's father violating some rule, and they shot him.

But Maniek, the oldest of the four Karbowski children, came to me to ask a favor, and I had to listen. I could not afford to antagonize him. Real vodka could no longer be obtained, so farmers made their own moonshine vodka and sold it in town in five-gallon tin drums. The Germans had forbidden the sale of this vodka, so Maniek asked if I would store his moonshine in one of our sheds. I gave him some storage space, and he came in from time to time to take some. When he was short on cash, I lent him money. Maniek told me I was his best friend.

As more and more Jewish businesses closed, there was no longer enough money for the *Judenrat* to meet the Germans' demands. No more juice could be squeezed from the Jewish lemon. The future did not look bright.

VI

During this turmoil, my younger brother, Yerachmiel, and his girlfriend, Itke, decided to marry. They had dated for three years, while Itke had worked making feather bedspreads and comforters for the farmers. After the invasion, she no longer was allowed to work in her home, so she lived and worked at the farmhouses. To keep Yerachmiel from work details, she hid him in her house, her relatives' houses, or on farms where she worked.

They wanted to marry. They did not know how long they would be alive, and they did not want to be apart any longer. The families agreed to the wedding, although my mother initially opposed the idea under the circumstances. Wedding preparations moved along quickly. My mother drew up a menu and calculated what she could afford. She bought fish from a Polish friend and made gefilte fish. Live chickens were obtained on the black market. One of our neighbors, a butcher, came over at night and slaughtered the chickens secretly in our basement to make certain that they would be kosher. Menucha plucked the feathers. Itke's mother baked challahs and cakes. I bought wine and whiskey, though my heart was not in it.

After eight days, everything was set. Because our rabbi had been murdered, the rabbi of Wyszkow officiated. He had been evicted by the Germans from his hometown and transferred to Wegrow. The wedding took place in a neighbor's house, because it was larger than ours. The "sanctuary" consisted of four dirty walls. I tied each of the four corners of my father's tallis to four poles to serve as a *chuppah* (fringed canopy) over the bride and groom. As people arrived, I saw only sadness in the room. No one said *"mazel tov."* The mood was that of a funeral, not a wedding.

When the ceremony began, my mother unexpectedly took my hand and said, "Bless my children." It was customary for the father to bless the bride and groom. I stood motionless. I had not expected this. In a time when we had sustained curse after curse, I was not prepared to offer such a prayer. I did not believe blessings still existed for us, but I did not want to disobey my mother.

Slowly, I approached the bride and groom, put my hands on their heads, and began, "May the Lord bless you and keep you." My eyes filled with tears, and I could not go on. The others in the room wept, and a sea of tears washed the room. I led the bride and groom to the *chuppah.* The rabbi raised his eyes heavenward and said, "God, give us the strength and years so that this wedding will not be the last among our people." Again everyone wept. After some time, when we had regained our composure, the rabbi concluded the ceremony.

The guests wished us a *mazel tov.* Everyone drank a toast to the couple and sat down to partake of the feast. In those austere times, we feasted on challah, gefilte fish, boiled chicken and chicken soup, sweetened carrots, and apple compote. The guests departed quickly to arrive home before the curfew. This was one of the last Jewish weddings in Wegrow. It was the very last one for a long time.

The young couple went home as husband and wife. They were awakened that night by several Jewish policemen who came in and ordered them to get dressed. They were sent to Mord, a village near Wegrow, where a labor force of several hundred repaired soil erosion caused by a small river. This was their honeymoon.

Back at our home, we did not want to be caught unprepared, so I made sure that we had adequate supplies in our attic hiding place. We stocked pillows, blankets, matches, candles, an electric lamp, and a knife in the attic. Every week I checked the food and replaced what had spoiled.

My older brother, Yitzchak, had made a hiding place of his own in the non-Jewish part of town. He lived there with his wife and two children, Renia and Eddie. Eddie, the youngest, was a boy of only two-and-a-half. Yitzchak had removed a few of the floorboards of his house, dug a hole beneath the floor, and hollowed out a small hiding place to hide the family for a brief time. Outside, in a firewood storage shed, he built a false wall leaving a space behind it as a secret annex.

Near Jarnic, about fifteen miles from Wegrow, lived a Mr. Tofel, a gentile who owned about thirty acres of poor farming land, a small house, one horse, one cow, and two pigs. (In Europe, everyone greeted his neighbor as Mr. or Mrs. so and so. We did not usually call each other by first names; to do so would have been considered a sign of disrespect. Because of this I did not know the first names of many of our acquaintances. Furthermore, I was still only a young man when the war broke out, though I had carried heavy responsibilities for years.) Mr. Tofel had a wife and two small children. He was a tall, slim man with ruffled, uncombed dark hair. He ambled slowly when he walked. He was a slow-moving, slow-thinking man, but hard-working and honest. His wife was a tall woman, perhaps six feet tall, with dark-blonde hair. A plain woman, she was shy and rarely spoke. Yitzchak asked him if he could rent a small piece of land on which he could dig a hiding place. He also asked if Tofel would be able to supply a daily ration of water and bread or potatoes. Tofel agreed, and Yitzchak asked him how much he would charge. He mentioned an amount and insisted that it must be in the form of gold dollars. Yitzchak agreed. He went on to warn Tofel that no one, not even his own family, must know of the plan. He told Tofel not to buy anything with the gold. Everyone knew that he was a poor farmer, and this would certainly attract suspicion. Tofel agreed. Yitzchak asked him to come to Wegrow to pick up some boards with which to cover the hiding place. They loaded the boards and went to the field to choose a secluded spot where no one was likely to pass by. That night, they both dug a hole six feet square and four feet deep. They covered the hole with the boards and made a removable wooden lid to serve as an entrance. The entrance was one-and-a-half feet by two feet. They covered the boards with earth so that no one could tell there was a pit there.

Shortly after, Yitzchak and his family left Wegrow for the hiding place. Only our immediate family knew of its location. If circumstances demanded, we would also be able to hide there, and as it turned out, we did.

We had several other relatives who, to our knowledge, had not provided themselves with a place to flee. I had two half-sisters from my father's previous marriage. The eldest, Frieda, married Jacob Baumgarten. After ten years of childlessness, Frieda and the rabbi had prayed together and miraculously she had given birth to a son, Avram Mendele. She had been barren for years and suddenly, like Hannah in the Bible, she had given birth. The boy grew and was treated like a prince. When the Germans conquered Poland, he was fourteen.

I went to Jacob and Frieda and told them, "I am looking for a hiding place for you, should the necessity arise."

Jacob answered, "There is no place to hide. Jonah, the prophet, could not run away from God. If God wants us to be destroyed, we cannot hide from Him. We will go wherever all the other Jews go. We do not wish to hide."

Disappointed, I went to see my brother-in-law, Hirsch Recant, who had married my other half-sister, Miriam. They had three daughters, Leah Bracha, twelve, Beyla, nine, and Liba, four. Miriam had died in 1937, and he had married another woman, also named Leah Bracha. Hirsch was a printer by trade, the only printer in town. He produced all the local government documents and was very learned in Talmud.

He, too, balked at the suggestion of hiding and did not think it feasible. "I am proud of the reputation I made among the government people for whom I printed," he said. "They considered me a fine person, but when the Germans came, no one ever bothered to ask how I was getting along or if I needed help. Is it worthwhile living in such a world?"

"Think of your young children and have pity on them," I pleaded.

He replied, "If God does not pity my children, there is nothing I can do. Do not talk to me about this any more. I will go to my end with all the other Jews."

"Give up on yourself, if you must, but you have no right to give up on your children," I admonished him.

He retorted, "If my children remain alive, they will curse me for not having allowed them to die earlier."

I was shocked to hear a father talk about his children in this manner. I was speechless. His disillusionment with his friends and colleagues in

Poland was so great that he insisted his situation was hopeless. They now shunned him as if he were diseased, and no one inquired about his health or needs after years of supposedly close friendship. Even these gentle and intellectual people with whom he had worked for so long avoided him, merely because he was a Jew. Perhaps he was right. Perhaps there was nothing left to live for. Maybe I was wrong, but I refused to die without fighting for life, even a life so pitiful as this. But now I knew that no one would save the Jews of Wegrow, not even the Jews themselves.

Meanwhile, Rachel continued to visit the homes of the German women. She showed them new hat styles, and she tried to pick up whatever information she could. Some offered bits and pieces and then asked her to keep it secret. She asked whether she had to worry about her two brothers being taken for labor to Treblinka, and the women said they should avoid Treblinka by any means.

It was clear to us what this meant. Farmers from the Treblinka area told of trucks packed full of Jews going for labor at Treblinka. They went in but never came out.

The Germans, in the meantime, seemed quite pleased with the furs they had confiscated. On the radio they boasted of progress all along the Russian front and claimed they were approaching Moscow.

In July 1942, we heard that the president of the *Judenrat* in Warsaw, Adam Czerniakow, had committed suicide. The Germans demanded that a daily quota of Jews be delivered for shipment to Treblinka. In exchange they promised that he and his family would remain alive. Unable to go against his conscience, he took his own life that night.

We then heard that SS troops were packing trucks full of Jews from Warsaw and shipping them to Treblinka. If they did not get on the trucks, they were shot on the spot. Some Jews who managed to escape were turned in by the Poles.

Rosh Hashana approached, but all synagogues had been closed. We planned to hold our prayers in small groups in private homes. The Germans delighted in inflicting their decrees on Jewish holidays, so we had to make careful plans. I went to the housing administrator. He said he knew what was going on in Warsaw but knew of no plans for Wegrow. He said he would let me know if he heard of any new developments.

When Rosh Hashana arrived, about ten Jews gathered secretly in the house next to ours. We wished each other another year of life, and prayed. The day passed without incident.

After Rosh Hashana, Rachel again went to the German women with new hat fashions, but this time they remained curiously silent. They said only that any valuables we had at home should be hidden. If she had any trustworthy Polish friends, she should hide her things with them. They would say no more.

When we heard this we packed our clothing, bedding, kitchenware, and silverware. We took some to a nearby Polish acquaintance, Mr. Pierkowski, a wealthy farmer and a volunteer fireman. He was a bachelor who lived with an unmarried woman, unusual for those days but not unheard of. She was ostensibly his housekeeper. He was a tall, burly man with huge arms, who stood more than six feet tall. He looked like a professional wrestler, but he was honest and we knew we could trust him. We took the rest to a fine woman named Miss Zelinska, who was the first woman dentist in town. About twenty-five or twenty-six, she was attractive, dressed stylishly, and liked to wear fancy hats. She was a good friend of Rachel and an upstanding person. I gave her some clothing—the boots and the pants that I had purchased included—and family pictures. Many of the pictures in this book survived because she kept them for me. After the war, she returned everything that we had left with her. The rest—furniture, housewares, store merchandise, and an extensive library containing many valuable and irreplaceable books—were left behind in the house.

Yom Kippur fell on Monday, September 21, 1942. Customarily, we performed the ceremony of *kapores* on the day before Yom Kippur. Symbolically, we transferred our sins to a chicken. This year, as we performed the ceremony, we felt that we were the *kapara*, the sacrifice, for the gentiles.

For the service on the eve of Yom Kippur, Kol Nidre, twenty men gathered at the home of our neighbor, Shmuel Moncarz. Our cantor was Yitzchak Szydlowski, the butcher and *mohel* (ritual circumcisor) of the town. He had been a lifelong follower of the Aleksander rabbi. In past years he had been the cantor in the Aleksander *shtiebl*, leading the High Hold Day services. He had also officiated in the large synagogue on occasion.

His son-in-law, Joseph, also a butcher, and his two sons Moshe and Shmuel, had studied in the yeshiva. They were at the minyan. Jacob Baumgarten and his son Avram Mendele were there. Also present were my brother Moshe, Yudil Rosenbaum, Israel Rosenbaum, Moshe Steinberg, Velvel Rosenbaum the teacher, his son Avram, and a few others whose names I cannot remember.

When the cantor came to the prayer *Haneshama loch vehaguf poloch* (the soul is Yours and the body is Yours), *chusa al amoloch* (have pity on Your creatures), he chanted with such emotion and inner concentration that he seemed to be addressing God directly, as if He were standing right before him. The entire congregation choked back tears.

I could never have imagined such a Yom Kippur. As I recall these events, I see before me each person praying, as if in a freeze-frame film. They stood next to me with faces full of sadness and concern, hoping that they might yet live to see each other the next morning again for Yom Kippur prayers. Before going home we shook each other's hands long and hard, wishing each other the good fortune of seeing another day.

We began our prayers early on Yom Kippur, so that if the Germans caught us and dispersed us, we would at least have finished the *shaharis* (first morning service). Shmuel Moncarz was the cantor for *shaharis* and Yitzchak Szydlowski for *musaf* (second service). He reached the *Unesaneh Tokeh*, which reads, "Who shall live and who shall die, who shall come to a timely end and who to an untimely end, who shall perish by fire and who by water, who by sword and who by wild beast, who by hunger and who by thirst, who by earthquake and who by plague, who by strangling...." When he came to this point, we all envisioned "strangling" as referring to having our lives snuffed out at Treblinka. We all wept so loudly that the cantor had to halt his chanting and could not proceed. We could have flooded the room with our tears. After 700 years, this would be one of the final services in Wegrow.

After *musaf* we called a recess, and Yitzchak asked me to go out to see what was happening. I met Rachel who had bad news. She had been at the house of the German commander's wife. The woman told her that she may not have enough time left to make her a new hat. "I am your friend, but I cannot help you," she said. "If you can hide, hide yourself. I wish you the best. I was your friend."

Rachel told me that she and her mother and two sisters were leaving for a small village to try to hide. She knew that I had a place for my family. She said she did not know whether we would see each other again, and we said a tearful goodbye. Here was the woman who meant more to me than anything else in the world and I had to watch her walk away, knowing I might not ever see her again.

I went to the housing administrator. He told me, "I can't give you any details, but if you have a place to which to run, go there immediately." That was all he would say. When I wished him a good day, he looked at me with pity.

I returned to the minyan. On hearing what I had to report, the men froze. Yitzchak cried out, "Let it be the Russians instead!" Life under the communists for a religious Jew would be horrible, but what could be worse than what awaited us? Another called out, "Where is the world? Where is America? They must know that the Germans are exterminating us. Why don't they protest this killing of innocent civilian populations? And where is the Master of the Universe? If You could create a world out of nothing, then turn it back into nothing now!"

We concluded our services, shook hands for the last time, and departed. I went home and we all broke the day-long fast, traditional for

Yom Kippur. We put the remaining food into our hiding place. At the slightest disturbance outside, we were ready to climb up. We heard the sound of trucks, many trucks, in the street. We could not see out into the town square from the house, and we dared not venture outside. We could not sleep that night.

Chapter 4

Treblinka

I

I'll never forget the day after Yom Kippur 1942. At four o'clock that morning I quietly exited through the back door of the house and cautiously peered into the still night. My neighbor and good friend Shlomo Przepiorka had come out to walk in the alley and find out what was happening. I asked if he knew anything.

He said, "A neighbor woman told me that no one is allowed to leave town. She left earlier to buy fresh milk from a farmer, but was turned back at the edge of town. Wegrow is surrounded by SS troops."

"Goodbye," I said not able to think of anything else. "I hope we again see each other alive."

I went back inside and told everyone to climb into the attic hiding place immediately. When the four of us had situated ourselves in the attic, I pulled the ladder up, folded it, and placed it on the floor of the hiding place. I closed the door tightly and braced it with a board. We lay there, anxious and fearful, for about half an hour. Suddenly, loud screams and cries shattered the pre-dawn silence. We heard the cries of *Schema Yisrael* ("Hear, O Israel, the Lord is our God, the Lord is One"). We could not see outside, but we were frightened beyond belief.

Soon came the sound of hobnail boots clopping toward the front door of the house. A voice commanded, "Outside! Get out! Get out!" We lay petrified. We heard the voice of our "friend" Maniek Karbowski saying, "I'll bring an axe and chop it down." Momentarily, an axe was hacking at the door. Maniek told the Germans, "These bastard Jews are still sleeping!" When the door yielded, Maniek and the SS troops entered. The soldiers yelled, *"Raus!"* as they scoured the store and the cellar. They pounded at the floor boards but found no one. The Germans left. We lay still as if dead.

I thought about how the Polish underground had deceived us. They had never refused to sell us weapons, but they kept stringing us along, and we waited in vain. In the end, time ran out. Zeynwill Szpilman and the others who tried to organize resistance could do nothing. They never received a single gun and were left with no means of resisting.

When I heard the voices of my gentile neighbors, including Maniek, encouraging the Germans and offering to help them seek out Jews, I understood how hypocritical and underhanded they had been. Despite the German occupation, they still considered the Jews the primary enemy. First they would destroy us, then they would turn their attention to the Germans. How stupid! The Nazis would enslave them and work them to death as they had worked the Jews!

I heard the cries of women and children from the town square just below our attic hideaway. The SS hurried their victims yelling, "Faster! Faster!" The screams of Jews mingled with the shouting of Germans and the laughter of Poles. Children wailed to their mothers, "Mama, I don't want to die! I don't want to die!" Everyone knew where they were going and what would happen when they got there. All day, the SS with the enthusiastic help of the Poles loaded Jews onto open trucks that sped off toward Treblinka.

We heard two voices in the house. One said, "They must be hiding in the attic." The pair hauled a ladder to the attic entry and crawled up. They searched everywhere, knocking on the walls. We lay motionless.

All day long the cries and screams continued. We couldn't bear to hear the voices of the children and their mothers. I wondered where yesterday's cantor was. I could not imagine the pain of one who had so earnestly chanted the musaf service the day before. Now he would be transported to the ovens at Treblinka. There would not even be a decent burial.

Dusk brought calm and quiet. We had no view of the street and could only guess at what was happening. Frost formed on the tin roof. We shivered, but I am not sure if we did so because of the cold or because of what we had heard all that day. Afraid that someone might be listening, we did not utter a sound. No one slept the entire night. We thought only of what the next day would bring. Our thoughts were interrupted only by the sound of German soldiers entertaining women and laughing loudly. Next door, we could hear Maniek bragging to his customers in the restaurant. "We sent away a lot of Jews today!" he exalted. "A lot of Jews!" Then the men in the restaurant cheered.

Some time later, we learned that on that Tuesday morning of September 22, 1942, the Jews of Wegrow and most other small Jewish Polish towns were shipped to the gas chambers of Treblinka. When they reached Treblinka, the trucks dropped them off inside the gates and they were lined up single file. They passed by an SS officer who pointed in one direction or the other. Most went to the "showers." The few who were not designated for immediate liquidation, had their heads shorn of hair, were tattooed with numbers, and for months were forced to carry out the grisly jobs of burying the dead and sorting through possessions. These were the younger and stronger. They usually died of starvation, beatings, or disease or were executed after only a few months.

The rest of the people—men, women, and children—were sent to barracks where they were told to take off all their clothing and leave their possessions there, so that they could take delousing showers. They were herded together, all naked, into the "shower rooms." But they were not showers. There were false nozzles on the walls. Once all the people were in, the doors were sealed, and poison gas was released. Everyone died a painful, horrible death, their lungs seared by the deadly fumes. Then the bodies were removed, the gold fillings were taken from the teeth, and the corpses were burned in huge crematoria. Nazi "doctors" performed agonizingly painful experiments on some of those who were not gassed right away. Those victims usually died painful deaths after only a few weeks or months.

II

When morning of the second day came, more trucks arrived and parked in the square. Again we heard the screams of men, women, and children as the Germans continued the roundup. Outside our house, men spoke in Polish and from what they were saying, we knew they were still looking for us.

Around noon we again heard Maniek telling his brother that they should again search our house. "I want to find those sons of bitches!" he exclaimed. They roamed all over looking for us, even in the attic, where they knocked on the walls and on the door to our hiding place. We lay petrified, afraid to breathe. We remained quiet for some time after they left, again fearful that someone might have stayed behind to trap us. Long after the Nazis had assumed we had left town, Maniek came back day after day searching our house, looking for us. He never gave up. When it came to hunting us down to have us murdered, Maniek Karbowski had infinite patience. Finally, he had found a job he wanted to finish.

All day long, we heard the Germans dragging Jews from their hiding places and loading them onto trucks. Incessantly, we heard cries and screams, pleadings to God for pity, and voices asking what He wanted from His people.

What was going to happen to us? How long could we lie hidden here like this? Would they not eventually find us? What would we do when our food ran out? We were terrified, helpless, and hopeless.

When night finally came, quiet pervaded. The screaming and crying stopped. From Karbowski's restaurant we heard the sounds of our tormentors. It was full of Germans. We heard them speaking, laughing, and singing.

I wondered how such people could exist, how men could commit such atrocities. They were taking innocent, defenseless men, women, and children and shipping them to their deaths. They were unmoved as women and children begged for mercy. Now they were eating, drinking, and celebrating as if they had done a good day's work. Was it possible that humans could be capable of such things? Had they been born evil, or had they become this way under some inexplicable influence? Look at a baby in a crib. Is that baby anti-Semitic? When does that baby become a Jew-hater, one that would commit mass murder? How could an unemployed Austrian house painter convince a civilized nation to exterminate millions of people? Why would a village of people collaborate with a vicious group of invaders to send their neighbors to gas chambers? I had no answers. I still cannot answer these questions fully.

The revelry from the restaurant continued until it closed. Then it was silent. Later it became cold, and we covered ourselves. Only three days before it had been Yom Kippur, the holiest day of the year. I wondered where the Aleksander Rebbe, Yitzchak Menachem, was at that moment. I recalled my father's stories about how great a man his predecessor, the old Aleksander Rebbe, had been. I knew that his descendant had been taken to the Warsaw ghetto, but now certainly he was no longer there. Thoughts of the people I had known raced through my head. I used to see them every day. I would probably never see them again.

And Rachel. What had become of Rachel? She, who was so brave and so admired by all. Had she survived? Would I see her again? Would I hold her in my arms and tell her everything that I felt about her? Was this too much to hope? All I could do was sit in stunned silence in a tiny hiding place on the edge of hell and wait.

The roundup continued for several more days. We lay quietly just looking at each other and wondering our silent thoughts. During the warm September days, the galvanized sheet metal roof heated the room, so that we choked in the still air. At night, we had to huddle close together for warmth. On the morning of the fourth day, I decided I had to see what was happening outside. I took a knife and began to scrape out the mortar between two bricks on the wall facing the square. It took a whole day and night of scraping, but I finally gouged a small peephole.

In the course of the day, we heard Fishel Chudzik's family. They were our nearest Jewish neighbors and proprietors of the restaurant that Maniek Karbowski had stolen. They had three daughters, Bracha, age eleven, Chaya, nine, and Hinde, five. The Germans had often come to eat in his restaurant. The commander of the German forces here, *Herr* Giller, also frequented the restaurant. He had befriended the children and had brought them chocolates every day. Frequently, they crawled onto his lap, and he played with them. They liked him and greeted him by name.

Fishel had hollowed out a hiding place under the floor boards of his house for his family. When it became too difficult and crowded for all of them to lie under the boards, he stole away in the night to a nearby village to search for a new hideaway. On the fourth day of the roundup and before Fishel could return, the Poles scoured the home and found his wife, Toibe, and the girls.

They summoned Giller, who came and hauled the four to the front entrance of the building. It was near our store, and we could hear every word. The children cried and begged Giller, "*Herr* Giller, let us live! You know us. You used to bring us chocolate. You used to play with us. You used to love us! Let us live. Please, let us live!"

Giller yelled, "Faster, faster!" The oldest of the girls said to her mother, "I want to live a little longer." Her mother answered bitterly, "No, you will not live because the world has no room for you!" The children screamed and cried as they were herded into the market place. A few seconds later we heard some shots, and then it was quiet.

I could not comprehend how this man, who such a short time ago had played with these children, could become so cruel and devoid of emotion. Even an animal will not attack unless hungry or provoked. Animals kill for survival. Only humans slaughter in this way. It is we who are the animals. What was his provocation? How could he have become so heartless in such a short time? After the war, they all said they were just following orders.

We silently wept. These children had grown up next to us. They had played in our yard and on our doorstep. When they came home from school, they would tell us what they had learned. They loved their teachers. They were happy children. And now they were no more.

What to do now? Would it not be better to simply go to sleep and never awaken? Had someone asked us at that moment if we wanted to go on living, we probably would have said no.

That night, we heard the voices of Karbowski, his mother, brother, and two sisters as they looted merchandise, carrying it through the back entrance, so as not to be seen. They pillaged the house for about four hours, and then it became quiet.

By now, we were exhausted from fear and lack of sleep. We decided that three of us would sleep while one stayed awake and listened. If one of us should snore, he would be gently awakened. Later, we would switch. However, we slept only fitfully because we were so upset by the slaughter of the girls.

On the morning of the fifth day I peered through the hole between the bricks and saw Poles walking around peacefully and contentedly. They opened businesses that had once belonged to Jews. I could see in their faces that they were satisfied, unruffled by the events of the last four days.

The trucks came again and I saw Jews being led to the square. Clothing on many of the women was torn. They had fought, kicked, and scratched the Poles, who hauled them from their hiding places. "Faster. Faster!" the Poles hollered. A Christian wedding was to take place that afternoon, and they did not want to be late for the festivities.

A child begged her mother, "I want to live." A man next to the little girl screamed at the Poles, "You are pushing us into the ovens. God will take revenge on you. It says in the *Siddur* (Jewish prayer book) other nations will take revenge on you. You will be slaves to other peoples."

Another small child clung to her mother with a vise grip, as if she and the mother were one. Suddenly, the mother pried the child loose, snatched the shoes from her feet, and heaved them at a Pole as hard as she could. I started to cry uncontrollably. At that moment, I could no longer look out.

But the woman throwing the shoes in the face of the Polish police showed true heroism. The biggest bombs in the world could not have made such an impression. She had resisted, doing everything she could do.

Repeatedly, the Jews screamed, "God, take revenge. Do not forget our crying and our children's crying. Again and again, they said the prayer *Schema Yisrael* ("Hear O Israel, the Lord is our God, the Lord is One"). But the trucks filled up with men, women, and children, and left for the ovens. I lay back and thought about Rachel. If she had a child and someone took her child to Treblinka, she would have taken off her shoe and thrown it at the Polish police. She would have shown her heroism, too.

The next day, I saw the dentist, Dr. Niseman, and his family with other Jews being herded to the square. He had had his office on the square for as long as I could remember. He was a tall, distinguished-looking man, with brown hair, and fine features. His wife, slightly younger, was an elegant woman, quite tall. They had two daughters, one a college student and the other a fourteen-year-old who was quite intelligent. Niseman was a gentleman aristocrat, who dressed well and who had assimilated as well as Jews could in Poland. The older daughter was engaged to the son of the electric company owner. A competent, honest dentist, Niseman counted many Christians as clients. He had donated a great deal of money for hospitals, the firemen's auxiliary, the policeman's ball, and many other community events. As I watched the Polish police, firemen, and civilians taking the Niseman family to the trucks for Treblinka, I noticed the younger Niseman daughter break away and dash to the side of our building. The Polish police gave chase, shooting at her. She fell. Then she got up and ran. They fired again. And again, she pitched forward, got up, and resumed running. Five times they shot this fourteen-year-old girl, until she collapsed into a pool of blood.

When the police returned to the trucks in the street, just outside our attic, one of the policeman said to another, "She was a strong whore!" As they herded the rest of the family toward the trucks, Mrs. Niseman collapsed with grief, her head on Dr. Niseman's shoulder. He screamed at the police, "You were our friends for many, many years. When you needed a dentist, you came to me and I gave you the best care I could. And now you have paid me back the greatest price for this. You shot my daughter, not with one bullet, but with five bullets."

He lifted his hand at them and said, "My hand should have dried up before I healed any of you bandits and criminals." He then raised his hands to the sky and said, "The heavens and the earth will be witnesses. The whole world should be witnesses to what the criminal Polish people did to the Jews in Poland." With his hand held in the air, he added in Hebrew: "*Adas, adas, adas*" (witness, witness, witness).

The Polish police shoved the Niseman family into the trucks, and they were taken to Treblinka's gas chambers. All day long, the words "*adas, adas, adas*," reverberated in my ears. *Al tishkechanu* (don't forget). I will never forget, Dr. Niseman. Never.

The sixth day brought another roundup. I saw three unmarried Jewish women among those brought to the square—the Zlotowsky sisters, Leah, Rachel, and Sarah. They owned a building in the marketplace, not far from us. In their store, they sold beer by the stein, and they lived on the third story above the retail beer establishment. The Germans did not know anyone was housed on the third floor, so the Poles showed them where the Zlotowsky sisters lived. They were middle-aged, thirty-five to forty-five years old. The SS dragged them to the waiting trucks. Suddenly, one of the sisters leaped at an SS soldier, grabbing him by the lapels of his coat. A second sister attacked him from behind, and they both gouged their fingernails into the soldiers' face. The third Zlotowsky woman lashed at a second soldier, raking her nails across his face. Blood gushed from the soldiers' cheeks and foreheads. The women screamed and yelled. The soldiers seemed confused. They could not shake the women loose, and they acted frightened by the blood that stained their clothes.

This lasted about eight minutes. At first, I was glad that the Jewish women had lashed out, but the Germans grew wild, throwing the women to the ground. Then they and the Polish police dragged the women by their hair to the trucks. I looked after that truck for a long time as it left town—the transport that took these brave women to the gas chambers. I was proud of their courage, but realized in the end that they, just like the others, would die in the gas chambers. The women had won the fight, but their oppressors had their deaths as trophies. The sisters, and many Jews, died knowing that they had resisted as best they could. But they died anyway.

A few hours passed, and I saw Polish policemen and firemen leading more Jews to the jail. I knew these victims. I saw the rabbi of Wyszkow and his wife, David Miller and his family, Jacob Miller with his parents and two sisters, the families of two butchers, and some others from Wyszkow whose names I do not remember.

They looked tired, and their clothes were torn and filthy. They walked with their heads lowered as Polish children ran behind taunting them.

That night Karbowski and his family returned to take our bedding, clothing, and whatever else they could carry. They looted for most of the night. I realized that they were probably searching with candles. A spark could easily ignite the house. We would probably not be able to get out in time, and if we did, we would be caught anyway. So we lay frightened, constantly on the alert for the odor of smoke.

In the morning, everything seemed normal. The townspeople walked about, business places opened, and children walked to school. The little ones laughed, played, and teased each other. The Jewish children had once done this, but I saw no Jewish children. They were gone.

Later, I saw one German policeman leading fifty Jewish men, women and children, four abreast, toward the cemetery. Policemen and firemen walked alongside to keep anyone from escaping. I recognized one fireman, Desczynski. He had worked for Jews and had been friendly with them. I realized that these were the Jews who had been taken to the jail the day before.

Desczynski told the families to support each other, because some were too weak to walk on their own power. The Jews, some of them prominent merchants, walked with heads lowered, ashamed because the whole town watched. The entire community knew them. Their children had gone to the local high school. They would rather have been shot in their homes than paraded through the streets.

An hour later, we heard volleys of shots from the direction of the Jewish cemetery. The blood curdled in my veins. The families I had seen supporting each other in the street were now dead, murdered by these bandits. The gentile Poles were not satisfied with rounding up their neighbors for the gas chambers. Now, the Germans let the Poles, themselves, exterminate whoever had been missed by the trucks to Treblinka.

I lay down and cried, the tears streaming down my face. I wept as never before. I don't know how long I cried but it seemed like hours. I could feel nothing else. My neighbors shot my Jewish friends a few blocks from where we had all grown up and shared an ancestry for hundreds of years. I could not think straight. I could not regain my composure. The room spun around, and the walls closed in. Somewhere people were enjoying the sunshine of an autumn day, where no war existed and neighbors greeted each other with friendly salutations. That world did not exist anymore. I might as well have been dead, except...except... except for the hope that Rachel was out there somewhere waiting for me. Somehow, I lay there quietly resting.

III

When it became dark we again heard looters coming into the house to remove furniture. We dared not make a sound, not a cough or a sneeze. They were in the house for about four hours.

The next morning, our seventh day in hiding, all began quietly. Later in the day, we saw Giller leading some Jews away. They were tattered and bloody, and their heads were lowered. I recognized my mother's uncle, Yechezekiel Schlessinger, among the group. He was a well-known Hasid, about sixty-five years old. He had been a businessman and an alderman in the town government, and was prominent in both secular and Jewish life. With him were his wife Annia and their children Miriam, Shlomo, Leibel, David, and Shosha, as well as the families of the children: Miriam's husband and three children, Leibel's wife and two children, David's wife and three children, Shosha's husband, and another of Yechezekiel's grandchildren, Aaron. I recognized another of my mother's uncles, Mendel Marcusfeld, his wife Freidel, and their son Moshe with his wife and his son David. They were all led into the jail.

Most of the remainder of our family was about to be exterminated by these murderers. We sat and watched helplessly. We couldn't even shout out our grief and anger. We each suffered silently with our thoughts.

We had little to eat. We had not bathed or even washed since Yom Kippur. We had no bathroom facilities. Our toilet consisted of a metal bucket covered by a board. We had to keep the bucket in the hiding place with us. Modesty was a luxury we did not have. Because we were eating so little, we could go three or four days without emptying the bucket. When it had to be taken out, one of us cautiously left in the dead of the night and buried the contents in the lumberyard.

We were cold at night. There were spaces between the boards of the attic that allowed the wind to blow through, chilling us to the bone. We were frightened when we again heard Maniek rummaging through our house. What was the use in our going on?

The next day we watched to see what would happen to our family in the jailhouse. Around noon, one German soldier, six Polish policemen, and six Polish firemen led them from jail. Among them I again saw Desczynski, who had been a "good friend" of Yechezekiel Shlessinger. He was now in charge of keeping order. Also helping out were members of the Dules family, whom we had known. They arranged the Jews in rows and began to march them. The policemen, carrying rifles, paraded alongside to make sure no one escaped. Polish children stuck out their tongues and mocked the Jews. I saw the families of my grand uncles. I also recognized Shlomo Zylbernagel and his wife and Israel Zylbernagel and his wife and son. All together about fifty-five Jews were led to the cemetery.

I stood frozen with my eye at the peephole. Soon, we heard shots. They came so slowly that I could count them, one by one. I ticked off more than fifty, not rounds fired from the Germans' machine guns, but the rifle shots of the Polish police.

The Germans could not have had it any easier. One German soldier would supervise, the Polish firemen would keep order, and the Polish police would execute the Jews. The Poles finally could fulfill their fantasy of killing Jews. The Nazis only needed to send one SS officer.

Although we could not see what had transpired at the cemetery, I later met the son of Chaim Naczelnik, who told me he had hidden in the attic of the mausoleum built over the graves of some distinguished rabbis. He saw the Poles bringing this group. The firemen gave them shovels and told them to dig a large hole in the ground, large enough for more than fifty people. When this was done, they were ordered to undress and sit around the edge of the pit. While they were waiting to be shot, Yechezekiel's grandson said, "What are you waiting for?" The police opened fire and murdered family after family. All around, Poles stood and watched. The clothing of the victims was given to those who helped cover the mass grave. Everyone left in an almost festive mood. Chaim told me that if he had had a grenade, he would have killed them all.

For several days after this, Chaim said, Jews were brought in groups of eight or ten, their hands bound. They were untied and ordered to dig their own graves. Then they were shot and their clothing given to the Poles who came to watch. Shortly after this, the Germans offered a bounty of two pounds of sugar to each Pole who could find a Jew alive and bring him to the Germans. The Pole would also receive the victim's clothing.

There was no shortage of Poles willing to participate. In the coming months, armed peasants scoured the forests. They caught Jews, tied them up, and brought them to town on their wagons, to exchange for the bounty. The more Jews, the more bounty. It was as if they were hunting rabbits.

In our hiding place that night we sat *shiva* (a period of mourning and remembrance) for these fifty Jews. We couldn't even say *kaddish* (prayer for the dead) because we didn't know if there were even ten Jews left alive in the city for a minyan. Only nine days earlier there had been thousands of Jews. We wept.

The next morning there were no more Jews to catch, and nothing more to watch. The Germans walked arm in arm with Polish girls. The Poles and Germans were partners, and they had been successful.

I doubted that the search for Jews had ended. They kept accurate counts of the Jews transported to Treblinka and to the local cemetery. They knew that our family remained unaccounted for, and we feared that they would be watching our place. Indeed, we heard people entering our building, walking around, and pounding on the walls.

We thought about Yitzchak and his family and Yerachmiel and his wife. Were they dead or alive? We prayed to God to look down and have mercy on us. "Hear our voice, Lord our God, and accept our prayers in mercy and in good will." We considered suicide, but after long consideration, realized this was not God's will. It was God who had given us life, and only He could take it away.

The next few days passed in much the same way. During the days, we sat glassy-eyed and just stared at each other. At night, we whispered among ourselves, but there was not much to say, only to wonder what was to become of us. No one felt much like talking. We heard occasional shots from the direction of the cemetery. We began to see and hear heavy armored vehicles, covered trucks, tanks, and motorcycles passing through town in the direction of the Russian front. Poles stood by and seemed not to know what was going on. Some of the trucks stopped in the marketplace, and Germans came down, puffing on their cigars and pipes, speaking among themselves. We figured the Germans were preparing to mount another attack against the Russians. We could see little evidence that the Germans were weakening.

Actually, by this time, the Germans were on the defensive along the eastern front as the Russian winter had taken its toll on the German Army. The Soviets, at a terrible cost, had turned back the Nazi invasion. The Americans had joined the war after the bombing of Pearl Harbor the year before. After temporary setbacks, the Americans had begun to drive the Germans out of North Africa. The war would last two-and-a-half years more, but we had no idea what was happening or when it would end.

We became weaker by the day. At night, we shivered in the cold. On the fifteenth day I looked out and saw the Wyches, the Desczynskis, and the Dules entering empty buildings looking for Jews. Later, we heard fifteen or twenty shots from the cemetery.

We looked through our peephole at the marketplace and saw peasants hitching their horses and wagons. The wagons were loaded with grain. Heads of geese and ducks protruded from crates. We saw eggs, butter, and cheese. Men and women walked from wagon to wagon, feeling whether the geese were fat enough. They blew on the rump feathers of the hens to see how plump they were. They tasted the butter to see if it was fresh enough, and the cheese to see if it was rich enough. They bargained with the peasants to get the cheapest prices.

We lay in our hell, exhausted. We had only dry bread and water. We had perhaps three or four days' supply left. I can't describe how I felt. We were condemned to lie here in hunger, fear, and cold. Only twenty feet away were people living and walking freely, buying fresh food or whatever else they desired, and enjoying life.

We did not know what to do. Did God want us to die right here of starvation, or did He want us to die at the hands of the Poles and Germans? I saw children returning from school carrying their lunchboxes. If only we had one lunchbox for our entire family! Our stomachs growled and our mouths salivated.

On the nineteenth day, we ran out of water. We had only enough bread left for one more day, and so we decided to try to get food from a nearby Polish family, the Rowickis. They lived a block and a half away—a man, his wife, and his two daughters, aged eighteen and nineteen. They had lived there and had operated their store in the marketplace for as long as I could remember. He had been a rabid Polish nationalist, and I was sure he would not cooperate with the Germans. We decided that Moshe and I would go out late that night, dig up some of our hidden merchandise, and take a pair of leather shoes to Rowicki's wife in exchange for two loaves of bread.

At midnight, Moshe and I opened the attic trap door. My mother began to sob quietly, afraid that we would be caught and killed. But we had no alternative. We cautioned our mother and Menucha not to make a sound, even if they thought they heard us returning. We devised a signal. The password was *l'chaim* (to life). How ironic! We carefully left the house and tiptoed through the backyard to the sheds of the lumberyard and dug up a pair of shoes. The hole was meticulously refilled so it could not be recognized.

The moon was not out, and we plodded through inky blackness as we made our way from the yard. We walked barefoot so that no one would hear us. The air was cold, and our feet were numbed by the chill. Keeping close to the fence, we crouched and waited every two steps to listen, frightened by any rustle or the slightest movement. It took us an hour and a half to progress the few blocks.

Finally we reached the back of the house and saw lights in the kitchen. We listened for ten minutes under the window before we were certain no strangers were there.

We knocked and Mrs. Rowicki, a small, matronly woman, opened the door. When she saw us, she acted frightened, thinking she was seeing ghosts. We calmed her and told her that we had come from the forest. When I gave her the shoes and asked her for the bread, she said she had none.

"Do you have any water?" I asked.

She looked into the pitcher. "It's empty," she said. She refused to go to the well. "I'm afraid the neighbors would hear someone taking water from the well."

I glanced about and saw a pot full of boiled potatoes still in their skins, feed for the pigs. I planned to steal one when she was not looking. But she did not look away. Saliva ran from my mouth.

"Can we buy two loaves of bread and a pitcher of water, and return late tomorrow night to pick them up?" I asked. We asked, begged, pleaded. She finally agreed. We left without water or bread.

Carefully, slowly, quietly, we made our way back home again. An hour and a half later as I prepared to return to the attic, I looked around the house and saw broken doors, smashed windows, an empty pantry, and rifled bookcases. My father's library was gone. The looters had taken everything.

When we signaled and then climbed up, the women reacted with joy at seeing us. But when we told them we had no food or water, they were crestfallen. Our thirst was worse than our hunger. Now, we faced a day without bread and a second day without water.

I then remembered that somewhere in the attic was a wooden herring barrel which I had placed there in 1939 when the Germans invaded Poland. The Polish government had ordered that barrels be filled with water and placed in attics along with boxes of sand to extinguish fires that might result from bombardments.

I searched about in the dark for the barrel and found it, still half full. A solid layer of fatty material covered the water underneath, but it was water. I plunged my arm into the wetness and scooped some water to my lips. It tasted like sweet wine. I was ecstatic. I filled a pitcher and brought it back for the others. At least, our thirst was slaked.

The next day I saw that the water had a reddish tinge, like wine, and small worms in it. It didn't matter. It kept us alive. We drank two glasses each per day.

But we still had no bread. Hunger gnawed and we thought of nothing else. We prayed we would be able to obtain bread that night and waited impatiently.

Night finally arived. Moshe and I retraced our path to the Rowicki's, but immediately I knew something was wrong. Someone was speaking in German!

We left and hid briefly a short distance away before returning home to report the bad news. The women nearly fainted. They had desperately awaited the bread and now faced another day without any. I tried to calm them, explaining that, had we knocked on the door, we would be dead.

How could that woman have done this to us? We had given her shoes worth ten loaves of bread, and all I wanted in return was two loaves and some water. She had been a lifelong neighbor and knew us as honest merchants. She had promised that our food and water would be waiting. Instead, she had arranged to have us killed!

Now there was no place to go and nothing to do but lie and slowly die of hunger. Visions of Warsaw passed before my eyes, how the Jews had looked when I had seen them lying in the streets, dying of hunger. Now it was our turn.

We each took a sip of water to try to quiet our stomachs. We had money with which to buy food, but no one to sell it to us, though there was plenty for everyone.

IV

By the morning of the twenty-first day, I was exhausted. I became very angry at my mother and wondered why she had brought me into this hateful world. I wished she would have strangled me at birth. Later, as I looked at her, lying crouched in the corner, I realized she felt worse than I. She had to look on helplessly at her starving children, seeing no hope for them, and knowing that she could do nothing. I pitied her. I forgave. Of course it was not her fault. Certainly she had the right to bring children into the world, because that was what God wanted.

That night, we had little choice but to return to Mrs. Rowicki for the bread and water she had promised, and so we retraced our path once again. We then crouched beneath the kitchen window and listened intently for fifteen minutes, but heard nothing.

We knocked on the door and Mrs. Rowicki let us in quickly. "You are lucky you did not come last night," she said. "Two German soldiers were in the house until very late. They became friendly with my two daughters, and the girls brought them home. They didn't leave until two o'clock in the morning. If you had opened the door, you would have been shot immediately."

I told her about our experience the night before.

"I have one loaf of bread weighing two kilos (four-and-one-half pounds) and a bottle of water," she said. "I was afraid to buy more because someone might suspect me of harboring Jews."

Seeing that an argument was useless, I said, "Thank you, Mrs. Rowicki. Thank you so much. We have to be getting back to the forest now. It's a long way."

We rejoiced at having something to eat, though we still were not certain she had told the truth. As a precaution, we walked toward the forest and later circled back, taking our time.

When we arrived with the bread and water, the joy was as great as if the war had ended. We each ate a piece of bread savoring each morsel. It tasted better than anything we had ever eaten. Then Moshe and I stretched out and rested from the strain of the journey.

Constantly we wondered what would happen. When we had eaten our bread, would we starve? How long could we exist like this? In the chill of the evening we huddled together, realizing that with each passing day winter grew nearer.

Then, my mother had an idea. She recalled an old friend, a gentile, named Mr. Dudek. A wealthy farmer, he lived about eighteen miles away in the village of Grodzisk. He had three strong sons. The entire village feared them, because they were such big, lumbering, powerful men. My mother believed that if we could get there, he would hide us at his farm, but I had never been to that village and had no idea how to get there. We could not simply go out on the road and ask directions.

I thought of someone who might help us. We had had a wagon driver, Jan Adamowski, who had transported lumber for us from the sawmill in the forest to our lumberyard. He had worked for us since I was five. Often, he ate supper with us at our house. A poor but honest man, he lived on the outskirts of Wegrow, about two miles from our house. Moshe and I decided to go to Adamowski that night and ask him to take us to Dudek.

It was dark and rainy, so we put on warm coats and boots, and made our way carefully through the fields to the outskirts of town. Because of the rain-soaked fields, traveling was slow and difficult. It took us two hours to get to Adamowski's house.

I knocked at the window, and he opened the door. He recognized us immediately. Adamowski, a middle-aged man who stood only about five feet, six inches tall, had long, bushy eyebrows and a tan, wrinkled face.

He worked outside all day. He dressed plainly and wore a traditional Polish cap with a patent-leather beak on it. He took us inside, and I told him that we were hiding in the fields, but that it was uncomfortable there for the four of us.

"We have no food," I said. I explained about Dudek and asked if he would drive us there, because we did not know the way. "We'll pay you well."

"I cannot take you by horse and wagon, especially at night when the soldiers can hear and discover us."

"Will you guide us there on foot?" He agreed. While we were speaking, a tall young fellow came in from the next room. "Who is he?" I asked anxiously.

"My son-in-law, who lives with me," Adamowski answered. The young man looked at us and said, "Since you are going to die anyway, why should someone else get your boots? Why not give them to me so I will remember you?"

It's raining outside and this is all we have," I said. He remained silent.

He went into the next room and came back carrying an axe under his arm. Frightened, I nudged Adamowski.

"Where are you going so late at night with the axe?" Adamowski asked.

"Out to sharpen the axe to have it ready for tomorrow's wood cutting in the forest," the son-in-law said.

Adamowski became angry and repeated, "You are going out to sharpen the axe so late at night? Put the axe away and go to sleep." Reluctantly, he turned and went into his bedroom.

Seeing me still upset, Adamowski told me not to be afraid, that his son-in-law would not come out again.

He then said, "Let's not travel side by side. I'll walk about 30 meters (a hundred feet) ahead. We'll be going through muddy fields, so we need to move quickly to cover the long distance before dawn."

We left. I kept looking behind, expecting his son-in-law to follow. After some distance I relaxed. We traveled all night, and I had no idea where we were going. We worried that at dawn we would be spotted.

With the first rays of daylight, we came to the bank of a river. Adamowski told us we would have to cross the river to get to Grodzisk. Five men stood on the other side near a small boat. Adamowski agreed to negotiate passage across the river and one of them told Adamowski he would take us across for twenty zlotys (seven dollars), but he wanted the money in advance. He also told Adamowski that Dudek lived only about 400 feet from the river. His house was white and on the left side of the road. We agreed to pay the money in advance. I gave Adamowski a gold bracelet for bringing us that far, thanked him, and said goodbye. Then I paid the boatman.

As the boat approached the opposite bank, we noticed the other four men talking quietly. We disembarked and walked toward Dudek's house. Two men followd. I told Moshe to run. If they caught us, we were as good as dead. As we sprinted, they gave chase.

We neared the house and saw Dudek standing outside. I yelled, "Mr. Dudek!" Help us!"

He recognized us immediately and told us to get inside. He turned to the two men and said, "Get out of here! These people are my friends."

"They're Jews!" they retorted.

"I know who they are. I warn you! Get out of here immediately!"

Moshe and I were frightened and exhausted. We collapsed on the floor of the house and lay there for about six hours. After our rest, we felt better. Dudek's wife told us she had cooked a pot of macaroni and milk. We all sat down together at the table, and I couldn't remember a more pleasant meal. It had been four weeks since our last hot lunch.

I told Dudek about our predicament. He was six feet four inches tall, with blond hair and blue eyes, and he wore a handle-bar mustache. He was the Grodzisk village president. His three sons, all honest, hard-working men, were even taller and bigger than he. When I was young, he would come to our store and drink with my father.

As we sat in the kitchen, we told him we could no longer remain in our hiding place, but we had nowhere to go. I told him that my mother had said he was our best friend and could save us by finding us another hiding place.

Dudek listened and then said that he would like to help us, but he could not. "When you arrived, the people of the village saw you. They know you are Jews," he said. "There are Russian prisoners in the area who escaped from the Germans. They are hiding in the forest, and I have been giving them food. The two men who chased you are some of these Russians. They are also searching for Jews. When they find them, they kill them and take their belongings. They go from village to village, stealing what they can. They do not make trouble in my village for fear I will stop feeding them. But I am certain they will kill you if you remain. Return home tonight. My wife has baked a large loaf of bread that you can take with you."

I asked, "Can you take us back with your horse and wagon? Moshe twisted his ankle while running and cannot walk such a long way." Also, I feared that the Russians might attack us.

"A horse and wagon will make too much noise, and the Russians might hear and block the road," he said. "My son will take you all the way to the road to Wegrow."

Late that night he gave us a giant loaf of bread weighing about 15 pounds. We ate as much as we could. Then he called his son, a tall, strong, young man.

"Take them to the main road," Dudek said. "Be careful and if anyone stops you or tries to harm them, do whatever is necessary." His son put on warm clothing and boots and put a knife in his boot.

"Why are you taking the knife," I asked.

"For protection in case we are attacked," he replied.

"Moshe cannot walk because of his ankle," I said.

"I'll carry him," he said.

We said goodbye to Dudek and his wife. We thanked them profusely for saving us from the Russian fugitives and for the food. As promised, Dudek's son carried Moshe on his shoulders the entire way, looking about frequently as we went. I carried the bread.

When we arrived at the highway, he told us to wait until no trucks or wagons were in sight, and then to cross the road quickly. I gave him my watch and thanked him. We said goodbye and he left. When it was quiet, I told Moshe to ignore the pain in his ankle and hurry across the road. We had to get home before daylight. Our lives depended on it. I supported Moshe under his arm, and we hurried across the road and through the fields. It was difficult for Moshe to travel, but he forced himself.

By the time we arrived home, it was dawn. My mother and Menucha were delighted to see us. I showed them the bread, and recounted the trip and its perils. Finally I told them that Dudek could not hide us, even for a short time. The joy turned to sadness. All we could do was hope for a quick defeat for Hitler, but from what we could see, this did not seem very likely.

V

That day and the next passed in the usual way. We had no ideas. We didn't know what had become of Yerachmiel and Itke or of Yitzchak and his family. At night it rained and the attic temperature dropped, but by now we had become accustomed to it.

During the day, many trucks passed. The townspeople left their homes and shops to look at the armored vehicles and read the writing on the sides. We could not make out the words, but the military procession continued all day. Perhaps the Russians had begun to push the Germans into a retreat from the eastern front! We convinced ourselves that this was the case, and we were happy. Was this really the beginning of our redemption?

At night the traffic ceased. In the quiet, we heard footsteps in the house and then a woman's voice calling softly in Yiddish, "Moshe. Shraga Feivel. Menucha. Are you here? It's Ethel. Ethel Prawda." We lay still so we could hear more clearly. When we were certain that it was really she, Moshe cautiously left the hiding place and walked to the other end of the house, so that no one would know where we were hidden. Slowly he approached her and recognized her. It was Moshe's girlfriend, Ethel Prawda!

Moshe came back and told us. I dropped the rope ladder down and Ethel and Moshe came up.

After a few greetings, Ethel said, "Our family has been hiding in the attic of our home and business also. After several weeks, my parents went down in the middle of the night to find something to eat. They were both shot, and only my brothers and I are left." Ethel was eighteen, and her brothers were sixteen and twelve. She knew we were hidden somewhere and hoped that our hiding place would be large enough for the three of them to join us. She had risked her life to come looking for us. Our hearts went out to her in pity and grief. We didn't have enough room for three more people.

"Stay here with us," I said.

She shook her head. "I won't leave my brothers. They are young, and without me, they have no chance. What will happen, will happen." However, she did remain with us for a few days.

We spoke quietly until morning. Again I looked out and saw German military trucks and personnel traveling toward Warsaw, away from the Russian front. Poles again stood and watched with great interest. How wonderful it would be if the Russians would soon defeat the Germans, and not leave one alive! At night we ate some bread and drank some of our maggot-infested water. Ethel realized she would not long survive on such a diet, and she decided she would return to her brothers the next night.

The next morning, our thirtieth day, Ethel wanted to look outside. She saw people going about their business. When she spotted children going to school, she began to cry. "Why can't my brothers go to school?" she asked bitterly. "Why are these children free and my brothers forced to hide for their lives with no parents and no food?"

Ethel looked at us, unbathed for thirty days, without a change of clothes, with little realistic hope of escaping alive. "Why do you struggle so to remain alive when you have no chance of surviving? And if you do survive, what kind of life would it be without parents, brothers or sisters, uncles or aunts, neighbors, friends, schoolmates, boyfriends or girlfriends? There is nothing to live for."

By the time she finished speaking, we were choking back our tears, trying not to cry out loud. Perhaps she was right. Perhaps we were struggling for nothing. The Jews who were already dead were better off than we were.

At dusk, Ethel prepared to leave. It pained us to see her go, but we could not convince her to remain. We warned her to be certain that no one was nearby when she left the courtyard and to proceed cautiously through the back roads. Should she be forced to return, she need only give the *l'chaim* password. We let her down, and we all cried.

I looked at Moshe and I knew what he must have felt. I thought of Rachel and how I would have reacted, if Rachel were climbing down that ladder. We were young men who once had hopes and dreams. We loved and wanted desperately to be with those we loved, but the Germans and the Poles took everything from us—our possessions, our hopes, our dreams, our love, our honor, our youth, our futures, and most of our lives. But still we had our God.

I kept mulling over Ethel's last words, that it did not pay to keep up the struggle with so little chance of succeeding. But what if we gave ourselves up? We would go to our graves that much earlier. What was the hurry? What should we miss if we remained here? Were we anxious for the darkness of the grave? So we lay another night.

I never learned what became of Ethel and her brothers. We never saw them again. In forty years, Moshe never got over the loss.

The next day passed and the day after that. We heard people rummaging through the house. What would happen if someone took over our house and business? We had an escape door to the roof, but where would we go?

As the days passed I tired of looking out onto the street. My mother grew weaker and began to talk to God. "What do You expect of Your children? If You want them to be better, then give them the chance. Don't destroy them. What will that accomplish? Give them a chance to repent. And if You are determined to destroy them, must You do it through the shame and degradation perpetrated by the Nazis? Must they be taken to the ovens? Must the Poles be allowed to take such delight in turning them over to the Germans?"

I listened to my mother arguing with God. I suspected that she was losing her desire to live. I spoke with her and told her it was wrong to give up. As long as we were alive, God might still help us.

By the fortieth day, hope had begun to vanish. We had enough bread left for another seven or eight days. We sorted through a list of our gentile friends one by one. They all lived too far away, and it would be too dangerous to try to get to them. We would have to sneak through town to get to them, and we would certainly be seen. No one had any ideas. The frustration was unbearable. Our depression deepened. We had virtually given up on the idea that we would ever leave this place free. The sounds of laughter from the restaurant next door filled our ears, ever adding to our misery. We decided that we would soon be dead.

On the forty-ninth day, the bread was nearly gone and we felt the Angel of Death closing in on us. No words could describe the frustration and despair as another day passed. Moshe and I decided that we had nothing to lose by returning to see the Rowickis. Perhaps, they would sell us some bread. We waited impatiently for nightfall and took the now familiar, painstakingly careful route. We listened beneath their kitchen window for fifteen minutes before knocking.

She let us in, and after a few of the usual questions about where we were and how we were getting along, I asked, "Will you do the enormous favor of selling us some bread?"

"Have you heard that Yechiel Kreda and his family are alive?" she responded, not answering my question. He had been the town launderer and dyer.

"The Germans have given him permission to keep his business open, because they need him to wash their uniforms," she continued. They had to clean away the blood from their Jewish victims, I thought to myself. "The Germans even took some Jews off the transport to Treblinka to help him in the laundry. They announced in the newspapers that any Jews remaining alive will be permitted to return from the villages and fields to town. They will be given food and allowed to live in the ghetto. They must work during the day repairing damaged Jewish homes."

"Are you certain that Kreda is alive and operating his laundry?" I asked in a skeptical tone.

"He is. I swear," she said.

I thanked her profusely, and we scampered through the fields to Kreda's place. We jumped the fence around the yard and put our ears to the window. We heard them speaking in Yiddish!

I knocked on the door, and Kreda opened it. He was elated to see us and asked about the rest of the family. He told us to bring Menucha and our mother immediately. We could hardly believe it. There were yet other Jews alive! We left immediately to bring the others.

On returning to the hiding place, we found them huddled together, crying. It had been so long since we had left that they were certain we had been caught and killed. We calmed them and told them about Kreda. He wanted us to come to his place and stay with him.

They could not believe the news. They were ecstatic. We all descended and carefully closed the trap door. My mother had not walked in seven weeks. Her legs gave out, so we carried her. At dawn we arrived, exhausted and starving, but no longer hiding.

Members of the Jewish hospital staff assembled just after the outbreak of war. In the second row at the center is the staff director, Dr. Melchior.

Guests at a wedding in Wegrow before the war. Noah Kochman, the Jewish chief of police who tried to arrest me, is second from the left, wearing a hat.

My girlfriend Rachel Man-
delbaum (center) and two
of her friends, circa 1939.

The Bielawski brothers. From left to right: Yitzchak, me (Shraga), Yerachmiel,
and Moshe, all wearing Star of David arm bands, as ordered by the Nazis in
1940.

From left to right, my mother, Sarah Freida Bielawski, me, and my sister-in-law Paula in front of our clothing store, circa 1940. We are all wearing Star of David arm bands.

Woodcarving of Bujalski's barn, where we hid in 1943 and 1944. It is one of several scenes that I carved while we hid at the barn. The Hebrew inscription on the edge of the carving reads: "In this place we sat while Hitler murdered the Jews."

Hinde Chudzik, the five-year-old daughter of Fishel Chudzik, who owned the
restaurant next to my family's store, and me, standing in front of my home. All
the Chudziks were rounded up and shot.

Sanitation workers standing in front of the *mikva* (ritual bath) just after the
invasion of Poland in September 1939.

The picture of my mother that was taken in 1943 for her falsified passport.

My brother Yitzchak's family, in a photograph taken in Wegrow in 1945, just after the end of the war. From left to right: a young friend; Yitzchak; a friend; little Eddie, Yitzchak and Paula's son; Paula; and Renia, Yitzchak and Paula'a daughter. Yitzchak is only thirty-nine years old in this picture; notice how much he has aged.

The photograph of me from my falsified passport, which
identified me as a Christian. I never got to use the passport.

Rabbi Jacob Mendel Morgenstern, rabbi of the Great Synagogue in Wegrow. He was the son of the rabbi of Sokolow. When the Nazis first entered Wegrow, they took him to the town square, made him clean the streets, and then bayoneted him to death.

The Jewish medic Nathan Weintraub, who treated me for typhus and saved my life.

Moshe Mandelbaum, leader of the Poale Zion, a Zionist organization that was active in Wegrow and elsewhere. He was not related to my girlfriend, Rachel Mandelbaum.

Chaim Worim and his wife. After they were taken to Treblinka, their two-year-old daughter, who had been left behind, was killed by an SS officer who picked her up by her legs and smashed her head against a wall.

A photo taken of me just after the Red Army liberated
Wegrow. I had been hiding in the loft of Bujalski's barn
for more than a year and had been slowly starving.

Hirsch and Miriam Recant. Miriam was my half-sister. Hirsch, who was a printer, was bitterly disappointed that none of his non-Jewish friends would help him. Hirsch, Miriam, and their three daughters died at Treblinka.

Left to right: Rivka Kreda, the wife of the launderer Yechiel Kreda;
my sister, Menucha; and the tailor Leibel Mazur's sister (whose name
I do not remember). All the Kredas and Mazurs were shot, but my
sister escaped by pretending to be dead.

My father, Meier Wolf Bielawski, circa 1930.

בית הכנסת הגדול
בוהגרוב

The front of the Great Synagogue in Wegrow. The Hebrew inscription at the upper right identifies the synagogue by name.

The sanctuary of the Great Synagogue in Wegrow.

A Jewish road work crew near the village of Sokolow in 1939. Jews were forced into labor gangs when the Nazis invaded. I am standing in the middle leaning on a shovel (arrow).

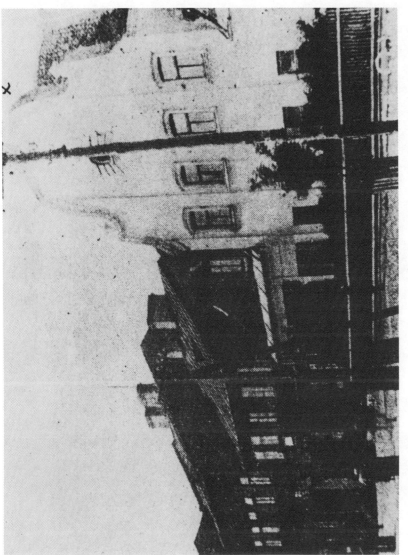

The building that housed the drugstore on the square in Wegrow. The building is more than 700 years old.

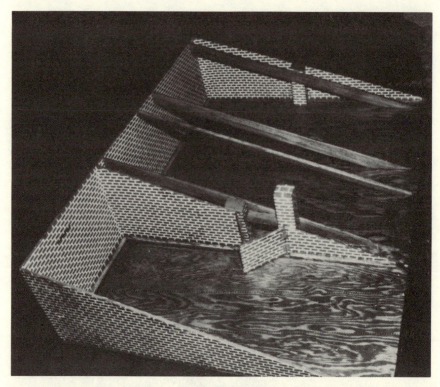

A scale model of the attic above our store and house. I built the door in the central brick wall (the door is shown open). When the door was closed, the inside area (the smaller area in the lower part of this picture) could not be detected. This is where we hid for seven weeks after the SS rounded up Wegrow's Jews for shipment to Treblinka.

The marketplace in Wegrow, circa 1937. The huge Roman Catholic Church at the front of the square is at the upper right in this photo.

Esther and me on our wedding day in 1949 in Bergen-Belsen, near the site of the infamous concentration camp.

My brother-in-law Morris Abarbanel, me, my sister Menucha, and Meyer, Morris and Menucha's first son, in Germany in 1948. Menucha is only twenty-nine or thirty in this photo, but notice how much older she looks as a result of her experience in Poland.

Chapter 5

The Story of Rachel

I

From the time he gained leadership of the Nazi Party in 1920, Adolf Hitler surrounded himself with rabid anti-Semites and murderous thugs like himself. These people followed his orders unquestioningly, carrying out his barbarous commands and overseeing whatever atrocities he demanded. One such Nazi leader was deputy führer Adolf Eichmann, an Austrian like Hitler, and a Jew-hater. Eichmann was in charge of the "Jewish problem." After the Nazis overran most of Europe, the high command pondered how to handle the Jews under German jurisdiction. They wanted to purify the Aryan race and rid all Europe of Jews. This they approached efficiently. They kept track in every area of every Jew and even went so far as to check people's heritages to make certain they had no Jewish ancestors. Anyone who had a Jewish parent or grand-parent was considered Jewish, no matter what religion he claimed to observe.

But rounding up millions of people and disposing of them proved much more difficult than defining who was a Jew. In the early years of the Nazi regime in Germany, many Jews were stripped of their citizenship and simply expelled, but this was not good enough for Hitler and his henchmen. He wanted every Jew dead, so the Nazis began a campaign of extermination in Germany. This policy was continued in whatever country the Germans conquered. They even pulled citizens of other countries off trains passing through Nazi-occupied territory, and if these people were found to be Jews, they were taken away to concentration camps.

At first, the Nazis thought they would simply shoot their hapless victims or starve them to death, but this proved to be cumbersome. So then constructed concentration camps all over Europe and experimented with various kinds of execution, until they decided that poison gas was the most efficient. Later, they constructed crematoria where they burned the bodies, because there were so many dead that they ran out of ditches in which to dump their bodies, and the smell could be detected miles away. In this way, they executed people quickly and without attracting world attention. Thousands of people a day were executed in concentration camps throughout Europe, the largest being Auschwitz in southwestern Poland. Nazi camp officials often filmed their atrocities in the concentration camps and sent the film back to Berlin to show their superiors what a thorough, efficient job they were doing. Some of these films were captured by the Allies when they liberated Berlin.

Twelve million civilians were liquidated by the Nazis, half of them Jews. Toward the end, as the victorious Allies marched toward the concentration camps, the Nazis tried to burn all records of their deeds. When they hurried to murder their Jewish victims before the camps were liberated, they took the children and threw them into the furnaces alive, not bothering with the gas. In some instances, when almost all the adult fighting men were called to the front near the end of the war, the *Hitlerjugend* (Hitler Youth) took over guarding the camps. These young teen-agers sometimes machine-gunned concentration camp victims who tried to escape or burned them alive in their barracks.

Eichmann was assigned to oversee the handling of the Jews, and he gave the order for the SS to ship Jews to concentration camps. He enthusiastically oversaw thousands of executions and carried out the Nazi plan of final extermination, the Final Solution. When Eichmann gave the order, the SS surrounded the area and the evacuation began. When these regional orders were carried out, Eichmann turned his attention to other areas. This is why Jews were taken to Treblinka from Wegrow on the day after Yom Kippur and why after several weeks, we were allowed to come out of hiding. Orders had been followed and, for the moment, the Nazis were not interested in murdering us—at least until new orders were given.

We arrived at Kreda's on November 10, 1942, after forty-nine days of hiding in stifling heat and freezing cold without proper food or sanitation. No one became ill, and that was a blessing. Even a common cold would have meant death for us all. A cough or a sneeze would have given us away, and any fever or congestive problem would have gone unattended.

The Kredas, to whom we were distantly related, were happy and relieved to see us. The rest of the family included his wife Rivka, his son Yitzchak, eighteen, and daughters Beile, sixteen, and Teina, six. Also living there were a tailor and his wife, Leibel and Sarah Mazur, their small child, and Leibel's sister and sister-in-law.

Kreda took us to his attic, where we rested for several hours, and then we bathed for the first time in nearly fifty days. Later, Rivka served a meal of meat, potatoes, and bread. We gorged ourselves on the delicious food. Never had food tasted so good! Menucha gathered our clothes and washed the undergarments, while Kreda cleaned our outer garments. After we dressed, we felt like we had been resurrected. We ventured into the yard to breathe fresh, free air for the first time in seven weeks. I saw the Poles from town bringing their laundry to the shop. They stared at us as if they were seeing corpses. We were thin and pale, and they had assumed we had been killed.

But soon we had to face reality once again. There was no room in the house, and we could not be seen in the laundry either, because only registered launderers were allowed there. If SS men found any unregistered Jews there, they would take them to the ghetto, where I figured Jews would be rounded up soon.

Because the Germans now needed some Jews to clean up and provide some necessary services, Jews were no longer required to wear the Star of David arm bands. We felt relatively safe walking outside because the Poles assumed we were all registered to work at Kreda's.

Toward evening, Rivka cooked a supper of macaroni with milk, bread, and butter, and again we ate our fill. We were not accustomed to such quantities of good food and the satisfying meal revived us, but we had to eat slowly and not too much to allow our stomachs to adjust. It was amazing what people took for granted during normal times. We were grateful.

At night we sat and talked with the Kredas. I told them some of what we had lived through, and they shook their heads saying they would not have survived. The tailor had been hidden by a peasant family in a nearby village. He sewed new clothing for them and mended old clothing in return for room and board. Kreda told us he had turned his business over to a gentile, who in return had hidden and fed the family at Kreda's house. We all gave thanks that we were spared, especially my mother. We slept soundly that night in the attic on pillows and fresh sheets.

In the following days, my mother had to learn to walk again, so daily I supported her as we strolled about the yard. Her legs gradually became stronger.

I kept wondering about Rachel and what had become of her, but I didn't have to worry much longer. She arrived one morning telling me she had heard from a Christian neighbor of hers that we were at Kreda's. We hugged, kissed, and rejoiced. "I knew you would survive," she said, but then explained sadly that her father and two brothers had been shot. She, her mother, and her sister had hidden in the nearby village of Krip, in the barn of a gentile friend. When they heard that Jews could return to Wegrow, they walked back to their Wegrow home outside the ghetto, where they were permitted to live because Rachel had made hats for the wives of the German officers. They were now the only Jews in their neighborhood.

"We are going to stay with Kreda temporarily," I said.

"Why don't you and Moshe stay with me in our house," she said. "It is large enough for more people now. I don't want to see you go to the ghetto. It is dangerous there. German SS can come in at any time, take Jews out, and shoot them."

I considered. We could not stay at Kreda's much longer, and Rachel's friendship with the German wives would keep us relatively safe. Besides, I did not want to be without her again.

"Thank you. Let me discuss it with Kreda. I promise I'll give you an answer tomorrow," I answered, smiling at her. She stayed and talked for several more hours before returning home.

Toward the end of our talk, she said there was something else she wanted me to know. I could tell that something was bothering her in addition to the loss of her father and brothers.

"What is it?"

"You know that I had to stay hidden away from my mother and sister, because there was not room for all three of us in one place. Well, I was lying by myself one night and in came the owner's son. He is about eighteen or nineteen years old. Big. Tall. I asked him what he wanted and he didn't say anything. He just kept coming toward me. I told him to leave me alone, or I would scream. He came closer. I told him, if he tried to touch me, I would scream as loud as I could and his father would come running in."

"Yes, what happened?"

"He stopped. He was afraid of his father, I guess."

"Did he touch you?"

"No, but I know he would have raped me, if I had not threatened to scream. I wish you had been there. I wish you had been there to stop him. I don't want to go back there. I am afraid."

"Don't worry. We'll find another place for you to hide."

Maybe the Germans would not touch the Jewish women, but I could see that the Poles would. Rachel had never been with a man, and this incident frightened her greatly. I knew we would have to choose hiding places for the women more carefully.

Kreda agreed that staying with Rachel was a good idea. He suggested that we eat at his place during the day and spend nights at the Mandelbaum's house. "I'll give Menucha room and board in exchange for working in the laundry, too," he said. "She will be added to the official list of workers. Your mother, however, will have to remain in the attic, until you can find another place for her." I informed Rachel of the plan the next day.

As the rest of November 1942 passed, we began to feel human again. We ate well, walked outside relatively freely, and slept in clean beds for the first time in two months. But we didn't believe the Germans would leave us alone for long. Moshe and I located the gold buried in the lumberyard and dug it up. We stashed the coins in metal boxes about six inches deep and reburied them behind Kreda's house next to his neighbor's brick wall. We marked the spot in the ground with a small nail pounded into the wall.

Rachel continued visiting German women to show her hats, and listened for talk about what the SS had in store for the few Jews who remained alive. The German women informed her about what they heard from their husbands.

The soldiers used the laundry constantly, and I worried that my mother would be discovered. For several days, I searched for another of our former wagon drivers, a man named Saszym, who had transported lumber for years. He was a tall, immensely large man—about six foot six—and he had a huge head with a long face and thick features. He had red hair, blue eyes, muscular arms, and wide shoulders. He wore traditional homemade working clothes—blue linen pants, a white linen shirt, tall boots, and a fur cap. He was simply a giant of a man, weighing at least 250 pounds. The ground literally shook when he walked. But he was poor, uneducated, drank heavily, and worked hard to scratch a meager living from his farm.

A mile outside town stood the small house where he and his family lived. He had two small children, and he owned a cow and a horse. Before the war he had visited us often, and we lent him money occasionally in exchange for future work. When I finally located him and convinced him I would pay him generously, he told me that he would provide a fine place for my mother and that he would feed her well. A few days later, I walked to his house to inspect the living arrangements. He took me to an animal shed attached to the front of the house. The horse and cow stood on one side. On the other, he had built a wooden bed with loose straw for a mattress and old burlap sacks for sheets. The horse and cow stood only a few yards away with their rumps facing the "bed." Manure dotted the floor, and the odor filled the building. During the day she had to stay in the shed, though she could sleep in the house at night, he told me.

I felt sick. This is where my mother was to stay! A proud, hard-working businesswoman, she had been well known and respected throughout town. Now she was to share cramped quarters with farm animals. I knew I would have to find a more livable place, but for the time being this was all I had.

I returned to Kreda's house and told my mother about the arrangements. She seemed disappointed, but she knew I would look for a better place, so she agreed to go.

Satisfied for the moment, I went out into the yard and saw a young man sitting on the ground. As I approached, he called, "Shraga Feivel! Is that you? Don't you recognize me?" I could not. "It's your nephew, Avram Mendele Baumgarten." I couldn't believe my eyes! He looked awful. His face was distended and bloated, his legs were swollen to the size of telephone poles, and his ragged clothing was crawling with lice as large as flies.

I couldn't take him inside Kreda's house, because of the lice, but I said, "You look hungry. I'll bring you something to eat."

"I can't eat anymore."

"What can I do for you?"

"Nothing."

"Why do you look this way? What happened to your family?"

"The day after Yom Kippur, my parents forced me out of the house to the forest. They said they could no longer help themselves, but I could survive because I was young. I went into the forest and lay there in the rain and cold. Then I went to the farmers at night to beg for food. At first they gave me some bread or potatoes, but as time went on, they stopped. Some went into the forest actively hunting for me and other Jews. During the day I lay in a pit without food. At night I looked for food, digging up carrots or potatoes or whatever else I could find. Often I did not eat for two or three days at a time."

He had remained in the forest this entire time, starving, unwashed, for nine weeks. Now he had nowhere to go but into the ghetto.

I looked at him in disbelief. Here was the miracle child of my half-sister, for whose birth the rabbi had pleaded with God. Now the miracle child had given up hope of living.

"Things will be better for you in the ghetto. I will bring you some clean clothes as soon as I wash them for you." He turned to leave, barely able to walk on his massively swollen legs. I watched him until he disappeared, choking back tears. I asked God why he could not permit Avram Mendele to live. He was God's very own.

Two days later I went to deliver the clothes and food, but he had died. I felt a deep sorrow for the young child, my nephew, one more sorrow in a long line that seemed to stretch endlessly back over the months and years, so that I could not remember a time when there was no sorrow. I remained depressed for a long time over Avram Mendele.

II

The next day my mother packed some extra clothes, and I took her to Saszym. When we entered the shed, she turned pale. It was even worse than she had expected. I reassured her that this was only temporary, and, as I said goodbye, I promised I would visit whenever I could. I felt helpless, but, at least, she was relatively safe.

Two days later a man came to Kreda's house asking for me and introduced himself as Tofel. My brother Yitzchak and his wife and children were hiding at his farm, and they wanted to know if we were still alive.

"Tofel," I said, "give Yitzchak our regards and tell him to come to Kreda's for a day. It is now safe for him to do so." Before saying goodbye, I gave him some zlotys for delivering the message and got directions to his house in Jarnic.

Menucha continued to work in the laundry, and Moshe and I paid for the meals we ate at Kreda's. Rachel learned that more German soldiers entered the ghetto daily. Anyone not reporting for labor was shot. We wondered if the Germans knew that Moshe and I were at Rachel's house. They might come in the middle of the night or early in the morning to get us. We needed another hiding place nearby.

Yitzchak had lived with his wife's family in the house across the street from Rachel, where in 1939 he had built a small hiding place under the floorboards. Now a Polish woman lived there, the widow of the Polish police commander, and Rachel agreed to ask her if she would hide all of us, if the need arose.

She agreed on the condition that she be paid six months rent in advance on the following day. We agreed. The next day I went to visit my mother. She told me that during the night she was allowed to sleep inside on a sofa. He fed her bread, potatoes, and milk during the day, but she had to return to the shed immediately after eating.

I consoled her by telling her that soon she would have a real house to stay in, and that the war would not last much longer. After a few hours, I left, telling her I would visit her daily if possible. I saw tears in her eyes. Back at Kreda's, I advised Menucha that it was impossible for mother to stay there much longer.

At Rachel's house that night she informed me that she had taken a few orders for hats, and had asked the German women jokingly if she would have enough time to make the hats before she was destroyed.

The German women laughed and told Rachel not to worry, that things were not so bad. We assumed this was good news for us.

The next morning we heard that Mordechai Zajman, the former president of the *Judenrat*, was alive. His wife and two sons had been shot by the Germans, but he had hidden. Now, he was *Judenrat* president again. He believed he could negotiate with the German SS not to enter the ghetto to shoot Jews, but he needed money for bribes. There was little money left. The Jews who had fled during the Yom Kippur attack had left everything behind.

About a month later, Zajman died during the night, apparently of a heart attack. He had not been able to accomplish anything with the SS, and perhaps the strain had been too much for him. I had forgotten that people could die natural deaths. I could not remember the last time a Jew had died of a heart attack.

A few days later, I visited my mother and found that living in the shed was affecting her spirits. I left feeling terrible, but when I returned to Kreda's I found him in a jovial mood.

Annoyed, I asked him what he was so happy about, and he told me, "A Pole from the village is going to learn the laundry trade from me. He wants to take over the laundry if the Jews again have to flee. In return he has offered to hide all of my family on his farm and keep them there until the end of the war."

"But what will you do if the police surround your house in the middle of the night before you have a chance to escape?"

He thought for a moment and then asked, "What choice do I have?"

"Prepare a hiding place for yourself and all the people who work in the laundry."

Again he pondered. "That's a good idea. I need to look around and decide where I can make such a hiding place."

"Do it now. Without delay. There is no telling how soon the place will be needed. You can't afford to waste time."

That evening Rachel told us the mayor's secretary had advised her that, for the moment, there was no danger, but that there was no telling about the future. In a week or two, tragedy might again befall the Jews.

The next day I again went to see my mother, and she told me she was not feeling well. I thought she might benefit from a better diet, but I was afraid to tell Saszym to change her food. He could simply tell her to leave. I told her I would bring some better food the next time I came to see her. I sat with her until it became dark and then left. I did not want the neighbors to see me visiting Saszym too often.

I was depressed for the next few days, thinking about my mother lying in the shed next to the cow and horse, smelling the manure, having no one to talk to.

Finally, Yitzchak came to see us at Kreda's house. We hugged each other and told one another what a miracle it was we were both still alive. After a time, he explained that his wife and children remained in hiding in Jarnic. I told him about our mother's living conditions. "She won't be able to tolerate it much longer," I said, "but I can't find another place for her."

"Do you know any farmers who used to buy lumber from us who might be willing to hide her and possibly the rest of the family?"

"I'll go back to Jarnic and try to find a place immediately. What about Yerachmiel and his wife?"

"I've heard nothing." We said goodbye and Yitzchak left.

I visited my mother and she seemed relieved to hear that Yitzchak was safe. She was elated at the prospect of another hiding place. Later that day, Rachel and I agreed that the two of us must have a place to run at a moment's notice.

The next morning, Kreda told me he had decided to dig a large pit in the ground on his property. We all had to help dig for several nights, so that no one would guess our plan.

This wasn't enough for me. I recalled a friend who had worked in the magistrate's office before the war producing passports. He worked at city hall, where birth certificates were kept. His name was Mr. Ratinski. He had a bookish manner about him and, because he alone had control over the birth records, he knew he had a powerful position. An educated man, he performed his job well. He knew everyone in the Jewish community, but he did not like Jews. Those seeking passports for other countries or seeking travel documents had to bribe him or he would take years to produce the documents. A bribe brought the papers within a few weeks.

I needed papers that verified that I was born to Christian parents and that listed them by name. I asked Kreda's former bookkeeper, an elderly man of about seventy, to approach Ratinski about the falsified papers and to ask Rutinski to meet me at Kreda's house. The man agreed. The intermediary returned the next day to tell me that Ratinski would meet me at Kreda's the next day. We met in a back room at the noon hour.

"I need Christian passports. Can you produce them?"

"Yes, I can do it."

"Will you also make passports for my brother and sister?"

"Yes, but I'll have to have passport photos of all of you. Have them ready in three days." We agreed on a price and he left.

At the same time, I realized that if I were to travel in gentile circles, I would have to dress in clothing like most Poles wore. I owned a pair of officer's boots, but I also needed a pair of trousers with bouffants, so-called "officer's pants." I went to a young Polish tailor who had made clothing for me before the war, and asked. He looked at me strangely and said, "What do you need trousers for? You are going to be shot sooner or later anyhow!" My stomach churned at his callousness. I replied, "You know that I was always nicely dressed. I've decided that as long as I'm alive, I want to be dressed nicely."

"All right," he said shrugging.

I was dejected. All the Poles took it for granted that Jews would be killed, and they couldn't care less.

Kreda had begun to dig the pit. I told him what the tailor had said and how much it bothered me.

He replied, "I'm certain we will outlive that son of a bitch." Kreda truly believed he would survive the war.

Moshe and I returned to Rachel's house that night. I told them I could get passports, if we had photos. She told me she wanted one too. I arranged for the photographs to be taken by a Jewish photographer, Mr. Spielman, who had stored his cameras at the home of the gentile who had hidden him during the roundup. He took the passport photos at the laundry the next day, and we had the finished pictures by the appointed time. Ratinski returned to Kreda's house three days after the first meeting, bringing with him laundry to be cleaned so as to avoid suspicion. He looked the photos over, said they were fine, and promised to return in four days with the completed passports. He did and I found the work to be professional. We had gentile identification papers, which could be used, if the Nazis did not challenge them. I paid him 200 zlotys ($70) for the work, equal to about $700 nowadays. Ratinski wished me luck.

I visited my mother again that night with some food. She told me that Saszym was no longer taking her into the house at night. He was afraid someone might come into the house and see her.

The next morning at the laundry we heard a rumor that the SS had come into the ghetto to Shlomo Laufer's house. He had been our neighbor, a wealthy restaurant owner. They found Shlomo in the house and his son Israel lying ill in bed. The SS asked why he had not gone to work. Shlomo replied that he was sick and couldn't work. The German took out his revolver. Shlomo pleaded with him to shoot him and let his son live. The German shot Israel. Then he shot Shlomo. They had been the only survivors of their entire family. His wife and three children had been taken to Treblinka. Now there was no more Laufer family.

A few days later, Tofel came to Kreda's house with a note from Yitzchak written in Yiddish.

"Dear Shraga Feivel," he wrote. "I have found a place for mother with an elderly couple. They are religious Catholics who attend church every Sunday. He has agreed to take mother into his house. It is about three kilometers from Tofel's. He also wanted an underground hiding place built for her, so that if the Germans come to the village, she could hide there. I dug a hole under the floorboards in the kitchen of this house. It is shallow, but mother will be able to lie flat on her back facing up toward the floor boards. I placed a table over the loose floor boards so that the hiding place will not be discovered. It took me several nights to dig the hole. I have sent Tofel to bring mother to the couple's house."

We had known the elderly couple before the war, because they had bought lumber from us to build their house and barns. Because their children had all married and left home, he had an empty room. Tofel wanted to wait until dark so that no one would see him walking with a Jewish woman. He first came to get me at Kreda's house. I took him inside to a back room, put a bottle of vodka on the table, and served him a nice lunch. We both ate and drank, and he relaxed.

"Can you prepare a hiding place on your property for mother, Moshe, Menucha, and myself?" I asked.

"It has become very difficult to hide Jews now, because there are so many young Poles searching for them. However, your brother and his family have been with me for a long time. They are nice, honest people, and my wife and I have gotten to like them. I am also only a small farmer and need to support my family, and I can use all the money I can get. If you will pay me the same amount that Yitzchak now pays me, I will provide you a hiding place. If the time comes that you need to be hidden, the place will be ready."

I extended my hand and we shook, both pleased with the arrangement. "Please begin work on it immediately."

"I don't have the cash to buy boards to cover the pit."

I gave him money to buy materials. "Now, how do I get to your house?"

I drew a little map based on his directions. I wrote a letter back to Yitzchak in Yiddish asking him to take care of mother and to visit her periodically. Then I explained about the deal with Tofel. Tofel agreed to deliver the letter and not talk about any of this to anyone.

When it became dark, we went to get mother, who needed no urging to leave. Saszym seemed disappointed when I told him I was taking mother to Kreda's place for two weeks and would then bring her back. He had become accustomed to the money I was paying him. "I understand why you are taking your mother out," he said. "This is not a place fit for a person and the food is meager as well. If you bring her back to me, I will provide her with more food and a better place to stay."

"Thank you. I am pleased to hear that. I'll keep it in mind."

We shook hands, and then Tofel and I escorted my mother out. At Kreda's house, I said goodbye to her.

My mother looked at me dolefully. "I pray that I will see you again," she said tearfully. I watched her and Tofel until they had disappeared from sight. A terrific weight had been lifted from my shoulders. I smiled all the way to Rachel's house and slept well that night.

III

As the secular New Year of 1943 approached, it was bitterly cold, below zero, and a deep snow had already collected on the ground, which crunched loudly underfoot. Rachel's parents had prepared adequately. They had collected firewood and coal throughout the summer, so it was warm and comfortable—certainly warmer than at the shed where my mother had rested. The secular holiday season is normally a festive time, so Rachel was busy designing new hats for the German women. They were still telling her not to worry about the future. Germans and Poles busily prepared for parties and balls; Jews furtively dug holes in the ground for places to hide. No happy New Year for us. We suspected that as soon as the homes were repaired, the few Jews remaining in Wegrow would be exterminated.

Kreda, however, was happy. He was making money and thought the Germans would let him live because he was the only launderer and dyer in the area. They needed him. Mazur the tailor similarly thought that he would survive because good clothes were always needed. As a demonstration of their optimism, they decided to throw a New Year's party and busied themselves cooking, baking, and readying the wine and brandy.

They invited us to partake of a fine table, full of food and with plenty of drinks. We tried our best to enjoy ourselves. At midnight we toasted each other and wished that we would live through another year. But I had my doubts. Kreda was being ridiculous. He certainly had a short memory. I didn't. The cries of those children in the square just four short months before still rang in my ears.

In the morning we heard rumors from some Poles that the Germans were suffering tremendous losses in the east and retreating. We had no way of knowing that the Russians would not be entering Poland for another twenty-one months. Just hearing such reports buoyed our spirits, and I began to think Kreda might be right. Maybe the worst was over. Still, I could take no chances. Although the police commander's widow got her monthly rent for the hiding place she was holding for us, I did not want to rely on only one place.

Rachel and her family needed somewhere to hide as well, in case we were separated. Gentiles from nearby villages and farms brought laundry to Kreda, so I asked him if he knew of a peasant willing to help.

A few weeks later, he introduced me to a Pole whom he considered honest and who lived fifteen miles from town. The man agreed to provide us with a shelter.

He returned two days later, and I went with him to visit his farm. It was cold and snowy as we rode to his farm, and the ride was uncomfortable. But I knew that if I found another secret location, it would be worth it. This trip was doomed, however. As he opened the door to the barn, a horse reared up and kicked me in the chest with its hind hooves, throwing me backward into an outside haystack.

Laughing, he asked, "Are you hurt?"

"No," I said, not wanting him to take any pleasure in my discomfort. "Where do you intend to make the hiding place?"

"Right here in the barn."

"I will have to consult with the others."

"I'll return to Kreda's in a few days for an answer."

"Can you take me back home?" It was now past dusk. "I'll pay you."

"No. I am afraid the Germans will catch me with you."

"Can you just take me to the road leading to Wegrow?"

"No." He also refused to allow his thirteen-year-old son to take me.

Something about his manner stirred my anxieties. I felt the same fear that I experienced when the young man wanted to sharpen his axe in the middle of the night and when the escaped Russian soldiers spotted us. He was going to kill me! I still carried the old German pass commissioning me for labor, signed by the Germans and sealed with the swastika, so I produced it and said, "I must be on the job in the morning. If I am not there, the police will investigate. Kreda will tell them that I went with you. Kreda knows you and where you live. The Germans will come straight here, and do you know what they will do? They will take you and your wife and shoot you. They will burn down your house and everything in it. Now tell your son to take me to the road! I will pay him."

It worked. He was frightened and agreed. All it took was the sight of the swastika. As his son drove me, I could tell he was anxious.

"You have nothing to fear. I will pay you well," I told the boy. "Drive faster." He cooperated.

It wasn't until I got home that I realized how much danger I had faced. Once again the German pass saved me. Later, lying in bed, I felt a severe pain in the chest. It was what I imagined a heart attack would feel like. I could not go to a doctor. No Jewish doctors were left. The next morning the pain had not left, but I had to go to Kreda's house to get food. When I washed, I saw black and blue bruises all over my chest. Kreda later said it was fortunate that I had not made a deal for a hiding place—fortunate for me and for Rachel and her family. He brushed over the fact that he had introduced me to this pirate. Of all the danger around me, wouldn't it have been ironic if a horse had been my executioner? My chest hurt for seven or eight days, and then the pain left.

As February 1943 arrived, we heard more news from Kreda's customers, via the Polish underground, that the Germans were losing the war. It was now a race for survival. How fast could the Germans round us up, and how long could we hold out until the Russians came?

About a week later, we heard that a good friend of Rachel was confronted in the streets of the ghetto by a German town commander toting a machine gun. Frightened, the man panicked and ran. The officer shot him down. We had known the man well, and the incident only underscored our uncertainty.

The fading days of winter stretched on into late February. As the snow melted, I realized that our chances of survival in hiding increased with the coming of warm weather. A man I recognized as Mr. Czyzewski from the village of Pienki came to Kreda's laundry one day. He was a small, middle-aged man, about five foot five, with graying brown hair, but he was a robust man who dressed well when he attended church. Usually, though, he wore traditional work clothes. Recognizing me, he said, "Hello, Shraga Feivel. How are you. I'm a little surprised to see you. Who in your family is still alive?"

"All of us. I'm happy to see you. Come talk to me when you finish your business."

I remembered that he enjoyed drinking vodka, so I asked Rivka Kreda to sell me a bottle with some bread, cheese, tomatoes, and herring. A while later, Czyzewski came to see me, and I said, "Come to the other room with me. I'd like to have a drink with you."

Rivka had already set the table, and we sat down. I poured vodka into glasses and we drank. I could see he had loosened up so I said, "We've been good friends for a long time. You used to buy lumber from us for your house and clothing for your family from our store. I would like to ask you a favor, a favor for which I will pay you well."

"What is the favor?" he asked. "If it is possible, I will do it for you."

I poured him another glass and offered him the food. "I think you are a true friend," I said. "You know that this is a bad time for Jews here under German rule. Things are going badly for the Germans on the Russian front, and I am afraid they will take it out on the Jews. We think that the Germans will eventually lose, but in the meantime, many more of us will be murdered. Therefore, I would like you to do me a great favor. You are not a small farmer. You have much land and many barns. If we need to escape from here, could you hide several members of my family?"

He thought for a moment and replied, "This is a time when everyone is paying attention to everyone else's business. If my neighbors or friends knew that I was hiding Jews, I would be in big trouble. They would think I had made much money from the Jews and would report me to the Germans. In addition, many Poles are searching for Jews in the forest and shooting them. However, I want to help you if I can. Give me a little time to discuss this with my wife. I will do my best to convince her that we must help someone in need, that one must save a drowning person if one can."

"Money is not a problem," I said. "We will pay whatever it costs."

"I'll give you an answer in a few weeks."

I packed the remaining vodka for him to take. He seemed happy and left. I thought about what he had said. He appeared more fearful of his friends and neighbors than the Germans. What a condemnation of his neighbors.

He returned two weeks later to pick up his clothes and immediately indicated that he wanted to speak with me in the next room. He related his conversation with his wife:

"I am afraid because of our small children."

"You know this family. They are nice people, and it would be a pity if they were killed. They are also willing to pay us well in gold dollars."

"Where will you hide them?"

"In the barn. I will dig under the wooden floor. I can close the barn doors and dig whenever I want. No one will know what I'm doing."

"Where will you put the dirt that you dig out?"

"At night, when the neighbors are asleep, I will load the dirt onto a wagon and dump it around the potatoes at the far end of the field. No one will know."

"How many people are they?"

"Three or four."

"No, no, no! I do not want to hide so many people. I am very afraid of the neighbors. Two or three people. No more."

Czyzewski looked at me sheepishly. "I promised her that I would tell you she is willing to hide you, but no more than three people."

He waited for my reply. I thought a moment and accepted his conditions. We shook hands. I put another bottle of vodka on the table and offered him a snack.

"When I return home," he said, "I will immediately begin making the hiding place. But I would like you to give me a month's payment before I begin."

I paid him. "Work as quickly as you can." He drew a map to his farm on a piece of paper.

"It would be a good idea if you go with me once so you don't get lost in the dense forest."

We left together and rode to the farm, where he showed me the spot for the hiding place. I stayed overnight with him, because it was dark. At the laundry the next day, I found a letter from Yitzchak waiting for me. Tofel had stopped by.

"Dear Shraga Feivel, We are all fine. I visited mother, and she is much more content in her new place. The Pole who is hiding her is a fine man. You should leave town because it is dangerous and unrealistic to believe that the Germans are going to permit the remaining Jews of Wegrow to survive." He closed his letter hoping that we would see each other again alive.

That evening at Rachel's house, Moshe and I reviewed our situation. We had Polish passports identifying us as gentiles. We had a nearby hiding place in the house of the commandant's widow across the street from Rachel's. Tofel had prepared us a hiding place at Jarnic, and now we had a place in Pienki with Czyzewski. We decided to hide our new "gentile" clothing with Rachel's friend, the Zelinska woman, who was a dentist. She agreed and said she would allow us to change there, if the need arose.

On our way to Kreda's house the next day I saw people going in and out of our store, and asked why. The German militia had plans to convert it to an army social club. I realized how fortunate we were that the club had not been readied while we were still hiding in the attic.

I told Kreda about this, but he was unimpressed. He just repeated that the Germans needed him and would allow him to live. Then he began washing, singing as he plunged his hands into the soapy water. The mood was not infectious. In fact, that day in March provided one of the most vile memories that I will ever have.

A gentile woman came to Kreda's and called me outside. I knew her because I had often visited her neighbor, Chaim Worim. "Promise you will not tell anyone what I am about to tell you."

I promised.

"On that day in September, the SS came into Chaim Worim's house, took him and his wife to the marketplace, and sent them to Treblinka."

She stopped talking and looked about anxiously. Worim's daughter, a two-year-old girl with beautiful red, curly hair, had gone outside to play, she said.

"The Germans saw her but didn't know whether she was Jewish, because most of the residents in the neighborhood were non-Jews. They left her alone, and the girl didn't know what happened to her parents. Later some neighbors informed the Germans that a little Jewish girl was hanging around their house. The Germans came and one of them took the little girl by the legs, swung her around, and smashed her head into the side of the house! Her skull shattered and blood ran from every part of her body!"

"I could not bear to witness such cruelty. I ran to my house and hid," she said, her voice cracking.

Suddenly, the room spun around. And around. And around. And around. I felt as if the horse had kicked me in the chest again. I retched and retched. The words screamed in my ears. "They smashed her head into the side of a house." A two-year-old. They took a two-year-old...

and smashed her head into the side of a house. I had known that girl. I had held her in my lap. What could she have done to these people? I don't even remember the woman leaving or what happened after that. Sleep evaded me that night. A vision of that girl floated past my eyes for weeks.

IV

My twenty-seventh birthday arrived on March 3, 1943. A man in his prime with his future ahead of him. I had nothing to celebrate. I cursed the day I was born. I did not know what the next day would bring, let alone whether I would survive the war. What kind of life was this? I yearned to see the fall of Hitler and all our oppressors. This alone fueled my will to live.

At Kreda's house that morning they all wished me a happy birthday and said that the underground reported that the Russians were pushing the Germans back all along the front. Perhaps it would not be long before the war ended. I didn't believe it.

I told Rachel that night about the rumors of the war ending soon. She didn't believe it either. She had just spoken with the commander's wife and been given orders for several hats. Apparently, they expected to stay for a long time. They said the war was going well for them. Rachel asked about the fate of the Jews in Wegrow. She was told that as long as there was work for the Jews, they would not be killed. Of course, this implied that as soon as the work ended, the Jews would be destroyed. For the time being, at least, we had to make sure there was work.

Rachel found a potential short-term hiding place a few days later. Some good friends of hers, the Potocki family, seemed sympathetic. They were an older couple and were staunch Polish patriots. Their son was a student at Warsaw University. Rachel told them that she, her mother, and her sister were the sole survivors of their family, and that the Germans would probably kill off the remaining Jews soon. She was willing to pay for a temporary safe shelter. Potocki said he pitied them and would consider hiding them, but he would have to discuss it with his wife. He said he would let her know. She thanked him and left. A few days later Potocki told her he would provide a hiding place, if the need arose.

I was very pleased with this arrangement. I knew that the two daughters would never leave their mother behind. I only hoped that Potocki would keep his word.

From time to time I met with some of my friends from the ghetto. Judel Zywica's youngest daughter told us that every day someone else died, usually from typhus or some other illness. She was fortunate to be able to leave the ghetto at night to sleep in a Pole's house. I told Rachel about the pitiful conditions in the ghetto. We wondered how long they could hold out, but there was nothing we could do.

Germans continued to entertain themselves in their new club, our store. Every time I passed by my heart began to race. I had worked to improve the building for two years before the outbreak of the war. It was my store, my home. Now our mortal enemies were amusing themselves in it with the local Polish girls. I seethed but could do nothing more.

At Kreda's laundry it was a day like all other days. He was busy with his customers. It seemed he had forgotten he was a Jew. The thought that he might be destroyed with the rest of the Jews of Wegrow did not enter his mind.

On Tuesday, April 20, we heard that the Jews of the Warsaw ghetto had mounted a terrific resistance. Poles visiting the laundry told us that two days earlier the surviving Jews of the ghetto had begun fighting the Germans with grenades and machine guns!

We did not know what to make of this. It was hard to believe that there were still Jews alive in the Warsaw ghetto. The Germans had begun shipping the Jews of Warsaw to Treblinka in July of 1942. By September 22, the day after Yom Kippur, they had all but completed their gruesome work. Only a fraction of Warsaw Jewry remained. We could hardly believe that by April there were still Jews there at all.

But indeed, it was true. The Jews had finally been able to purchase a few meager weapons from the Polish underground, had hidden themselves in buildings, and had exchanged fire with the Nazis when the Germans entered the ghetto to haul them away. The Nazis vowed to rid Warsaw of Jews by the end of April, but still the Jews fought on. The Germans sent in the Jewish police first, then the Polish police, and then followed behind in tanks and armored vehicles. When the ghetto survivors opened fire, the Germans leveled the building with tank blasts. Still, the plucky Jews just moved from building to building, surviving in the rubble, and holding off an entire German division for almost two months. When the Jews tried to escape through the sewers, the Germans filled the sewers with deadly gas. The Nazi swine were made to pay for their roundup, but in the end the entire ghetto was cleared. Only a few Jews of the original hundreds of thousands escaped.

We were frightened, as was everyone else at Kreda's. We continued hearing that the Jews of Warsaw were fighting very well and even destroying German tanks. How was this possible? The German Army was the most powerful in the world. How could they be held at bay? Where did the Jews get their arms? Nothing of the uprising was written in the newspaper, but we continued to hear news of it from Poles. We began to believe it was really true.

Rachel's customers said they knew nothing of the uprising. We were still also hearing that the Germans were doing badly on the Russian front. Yet there was nothing in the newspaper.

I was worried that the Germans might kill the remaining Jews of Wegrow in retaliation for the Warsaw uprising. I told Rachel to make sure the widow across the street still had a place ready.

Moshe and I dug up some of the gold hidden next to Kreda's property. We sewed several of the coins into the waist lining of our pants in the privacy of Rachel's house. We had previously sewn some gold into the lining of mother's dress before she had left Kreda's. If we had to leave in an instant, we would have something on which we could live.

I was concerned also that Kreda had not changed his attitude. It was bad enough that he was endangering his own life, but he was also responsible for the other eighteen Jews at his place. When there was a lull in the work, I took Kreda aside and said, "Wake up and remember you are a Jew. You'll be killed with the others. You have no right to neglect the safety of your family and all those who work for you. It is imperative that you be prepared for the worst." After some time it seemed I was beginning to get through to him.

I told Menucha to be wary, especially at night, for anything suspicious. Whenever I saw anyone from the ghetto, I also warned him to be especially alert during the coming days.

We continued to hear of the Jewish resistance for several days. On April 25, we heard that the Jews were manufacturing their own grenades and firebombs and were killing German soldiers and destroying German tanks. We were elated that somehow these Jews were able to fight back instead of being herded to the ovens. But we feared the Germans would take this opportunity to complete their annihilation of all Polish Jewry.

The next day Rachel went to see a friend of hers who was now the secretary of the German mayor of Wegrow.

Rachel modeled some hats for her. The woman told her that she might not be able to finish making them. Rachel asked what she meant. She swore Rachel to secrecy and told her that something was going to happen that night. She advised Rachel to do something that night to save herself. Rachel thanked her and left very upset.

She came immediately to the laundry and told me what had happened. I began to quake with fear. I called Kreda aside and told him. At first he also was frightened, but soon he calmed down. He said he didn't think it would be as bad as I thought. I warned him that no one should sleep that night and that they be prepared to flee at the first sign of anything unusual. I found Menucha and told her to be ready to run for hiding.

Judel Zywica's daughter was in the laundry, and I told her what might happen that night. I asked her to tell the others in the ghetto. She returned an hour later and told me she had delivered the message. But the Jews there had no place to which to run or hide. They had no money for food. If anyone should escape, how would he survive?

When it became dark I said goodbye to Menucha, Kreda, and the others. Moshe and I went back to Rachel's house. Zywica's daughter went part of the way with us until she reached the Polish house where she was sleeping. She said goodbye very emotionally, crying and expressing the hope that we would yet see each other again.

We came to Rachel's, and I told everyone to remain dressed. I stood guard. We all agreed that at the first sign of trouble, we would leave the house, taking nothing with us, and go to the commander's widow's house across the street. I turned off the light and opened the windows a bit on each side of the house so that I could hear any outside noise.

Then I waited. All night I remained up struggling to stay alert. I could see in all directions around the house, but the night was still, and all seemed peaceful.

V

At dawn, I was jerked to attention by the crack of machine-gun fire from the direction of the ghetto! I yelled for everyone to leave the house immediately, and we dashed across the street. The widow opened the door to our knocks, but said we could not come in! Instead she pointed to a ladder on the side of the house leading to the attic. She told us to go up there. She would thus be able to tell the Germans that she knew nothing of our presence.

The attic was open and easily accessible with little security. But we had no choice and quickly ascended. No sooner had we scrambled up the ladder than the German SS approached. We peered through the cracks of the wooden gable and saw four of them. They were helmeted and carrying machine guns. The Polish police, carrying guns, followed, and then came twenty or thirty Polish youths.

They surrounded Rachel's house, knocked out the windows with the butts of their machine guns, and shouted, "Outside! Get out! Get out!" They waited a few minutes and then sent the Polish police in, but the house was vacant. Systematically, the soldiers and police questioned neighbors. We saw a neighbor motioning across the street. They divided into two groups, one group going down one side of the street and the other down the other side, investigating each house carefully and methodically.

We had nowhere else to hide. We were in this open attic. All they had to do was climb up a few rungs of the ladder and they would spot us immediately. We were terrified! Rachel stood next to me and held on trembling. I looked at her and was shocked by how she looked, faced with death. The poor diet of the last few years and the strain had taken a toll. Her face was dusky, and her skin had become coarse and lumpy. I frantically glanced around the attic looking for anything I could use as a weapon. There was nothing.

By now, the soldiers had searched the entire street and approached the widow's house, the last one on the block. We were certain this was our end. Silently, I said the *Schema* ("Hear, O Israel, the Lord is our God, the Lord is One"). We had fought, but now we had lost. We would be just another group of Jews from Wegrow killed by the Nazi invaders. Death was just a few ladder rungs away. Not even the Lord God could save us!

As we watched, we heard one of them say, "Let's go. They must have run away long ago." They turned around and left.

We stood motionless, mesmerized. Rachel's grip on me was so tight that I could not pry it loose. After several minutes we went to a corner and lay down together. We lay for several hours, exhausted, none of us moving or speaking.

When we regained our composure, we discussed what we could do about the widow's refusing us the hiding place for which we had paid in advance for six months. She was gone from the house the entire day. When evening came, we heard her returning, but she did not come up to us.

Later in the evening she approached quietly.

"I've been in town all day trying to find out what happened. The Jews in the ghetto have been shot. The ghetto has been cleared."

"What about Kreda and all the people at his place."

"I don't know for certain, but the rumor is that they too have all been shot." If this were true, then Menucha must also be dead!

Late that night the widow allowed us into the house, permitted us to wash, and gave us something to eat—bread, milk, and tea. Afterward, she lifted up two boards in the kitchen floor and told us to get into the hole. This was, of course, the hole that Yitzchak had dug in 1939.

The hole was six feet wide and two-and-a-half feet deep. It had been barely tolerable for Yitzchak, his wife, and their two small children. Now, there were five adults, and Rachel's mother was a large woman. We arranged ourselves side by side in the pit like bread going into the oven for baking, Rachel's mother first, then her sister, then Rachel. I was next, but there was not enough width left for Moshe. He therefore lay crosswise at our feet. We lay on our backs, face up. The widow replaced the floorboards and placed the table over them.

We were miserable packed into the shallow hole like sardines. When the widow walked above, fine sand and dirt fell through the cracks and stung our hot, sweaty faces. The dirt stuck. We tried to brush it off, but it chafed our skin like sandpaper. We could not move our legs and developed cramps in our calves and thighs. We tried to rub our legs to make them feel better, but there was barely enough room to do even this. We lay this way all night.

Aside from our terrible physical discomfort, we were too frightened to sleep. What had happened to Menucha? No one slept. We barely breathed.

At daybreak the widow spoke to us through the boards. "I'm going out to shop for food for you. Remain very still if someone should come in while I'm gone. I'll tap the floor twice with a stick when I return so that you'll know that it is me."

"Find out from his neighbors what happened to Kreda. You can go over there on the pretext that you left some laundry with him."

"All right, I'll see what I can learn." She left.

She returned in the afternoon and gave us the signal. She fed us bread with butter, milk, and tea. "Kreda, his wife, and their two children have been shot. The Germans and Poles also shot everyone else who had worked there . . . except for one girl, Menucha Bielawski. They shot at her as she escaped, but somehow she made it out alive." I was overjoyed but could hardly believe it was true.

That night we again lay face up in the hole, the sand falling on our faces. Again we had difficulty sleeping. These conditions were intolerable; we would not last long in such circumstances.

In the morning the widow lifted one of the floorboards and peered in as if to see if we were still alive. She told us she was going out until noon. I asked her to try to find out about Menucha, and she said she would.

She came back several hours and later and knocked twice on the floor. We eagerly awaited any news, but she occupied herself in the house for about an hour. Finally she lifted up one board and handed us some bread and tea.

"Kreda's family is dead, except for one son, who had slept elsewhere. Menucha apparently was shot and fell to the ground. They took her for dead, but when the police left, she got up and escaped. It is rumored that she went to the place where her mother is hiding. All the Jews of the ghetto are dead. There are no Jews left in Wegrow."

We lay still—depressed, numb. I was relieved that Menucha had escaped, but all the Jews of Wegrow were gone. All of them! We spoke quietly to one another and wondered if life were worth living. Maybe the dead Jews were better off. They had died quickly. Lying here in this tomb, we were dying little by little.

After we had another night of fitful sleep, the widow came and told us she was afraid someone would find out that she was hiding Jews. We had to leave immediately! I pleaded, "Must it be today? Couldn't we stay just one more day?"

She replied emphatically, "No, you must leave tonight!" She replaced the board and left.

This was our third day in her house. We had paid rent in advance for six months, and now she was allowing us to stay for three days! I suggested we go to Saszym for two reasons—Menucha may have gone there, since he had hidden my mother there once and Saszym knew us. The barn with the animals would not be a pleasant place, but it was better than hiding near the street until the SS found us.

We decided to leave at about eleven that night. The widow's house was on Kozia Street. We would go along Sokolow Street to the rye mill of Mendel Klein, cross the Struga River, follow the river bank west to Starowiejska Street, and turn and walk to the slaughterhouse near Saszym's place.

At ten, we emerged stiffly from the hole and washed ourselves—first the women, then Moshe and I. We were exhausted, but we strained ourselves to move as quickly as possible. The widow gave us a five-pound loaf of bread.

At eleven, I checked outside. It was dark, and a heavy rain was falling. When I was sure no one was outside, we said goodbye to the widow, thanked her, and darted outside.

We crept along Sokolow Street, huddling close to the walls, because many Germans lived there. We passed the Russian Church and approached Klein's mill. Dogs barked as we approached so we took a longer route around them. We came to the river. What now? We could not use the bridge at the mill, because the mill had been taken over by a *Volksdeutsch*. He would not hesitate to shoot us.

We had to ford the twenty-foot-wide river. The water came to my hips. Moshe, Rachel, and her sister crossed without difficulty. Rachel's mother weighed about 190 pounds, and was afraid of the freezing water. I hoisted her to my shoulders and waded into the river, but my feet sank into the mud, and I couldn't pull them out. Quietly, I called to the others to come back and take Mrs. Mandelbaum off my shoulders. My legs were numb and stiff from the icy water. Moshe freed my feet and the three helped Mrs. Mandelbaum walk across. I followed and collapsed on the opposite shore, rubbing my knees briskly to circulate the blood and bring some feeling back.

We had little time to dawdle, because we didn't want any passers-by to spot us. Quickly, we walked toward Saszym's house. The exertion warmed me, and it became easier to move my legs. By one o'clock we reached the slaughterhouse, which was only a few blocks from Saszym's.

Saszym's home was small and had low windows. It was still drizzling.

Moshe and I approached, while the women stayed behind a short distance. I tapped on a window, but no one answered. I called his name, knocked again, and said who I was. Again no answer. I stood and waited fifteen minutes.

Finally, I heard a stirring inside and the outside door open. Suddenly, a hand yanked my collar and dragged me backward. Simultaneously, I felt a sharp blow on my arm. Saszym had come out of the house and swung a large club at my head, but Moshe had pulled me out of the way. The club landed solidly on my arm instead of my skull. My arm swelled immediately.

We ran, but Saszym pursued us. We ran harder, and I yelled, "Saszym, don't you know me? I'm Feivel Bielawski! You remember me. You used to work for us. You used to come to our house and eat with us. Why do you want to kill us?" He did not answer, but continued to chase us. Finally, after about a half mile, he stopped and went back to his house.

We stopped to catch our breath. What was happening? Perhaps Menucha had come to him and he had killed her. Maybe that was why he had tried to kill us.

After several minutes I called to Rachel. It was too dark to see, but they followed my voice and found us. They had heard Saszym chasing us, so they hid behind the house until he went inside.

Now what? Rachel suggested that we go to the Schultz house, fifteen blocks away in a German neighborhood, to the woman who had warned Rachel to hide. There was a large tree-lined garden area behind the house, surrounded by a tall wooden fence. We hurried in that direction. Rachel knew her mother could not travel much farther, but she would not leave her behind. Perhaps the women would be able to stay there for a short time. From there they could go to another hiding place.

When we got to the house, I tore off two boards from the garden fence, and we scrambled through. Rachel knocked. The door opened and she disappeared through the doorway. Impatiently, we waited. Five. Ten. Fifteen. Twenty minutes passed. No Rachel. At best, only the women would be able to stay here. Moshe and I still had to try to get to Czyzewski's house in Pienki, eighteen miles away through dense, unfamiliar forest. We had to travel by dark, and time was growing short.

Perhaps there had been a German in the house. What to do? We asked Rachel's mother and sister if they could make the trip to Pienki. Mrs. Mandelbaum said she could not walk another step. She could barely stand. "Save your own lives and don't wait any longer," she said. I gave them the loaf of bread, we said goodbye, and told each other we hoped we would see one another again.

We ran. We came upon Peretz Prawda's house, and Moshe wanted to stop and see if his girlfriend were still there. We quietly climbed up to the attic and found Moshe Mandelbaum (no relation to Rachel) there alive. He had been the leader of the left-wing Poale Zion party in We-grow, a Zionist organization that sought to establish a liberal, Jewish government in Palestine. It was the forerunner of the current Israeli Labor Party. He had been a Wegrow alderman, and a member of the Jewish Community Council.

"Where are you going?" he asked.

"To the forest."

"I wish I could go with you, but I can't run anymore."

"Do you know if any of the Prawdas are still alive?"

"I have not seen any of the family."

"Well, good luck, Moshe. Goodbye."

We continued running through the fields to the Jarnicer forest. We plunged into the thick woods and continued to trot on and off all night. We weren't even sure if we were headed toward Czyzewski's house or running in circles.

As the faint blue of morning lit the sky, I had no idea where we were. Moshe's strength flagged. I looked at him and saw a white foam around his lips, as one sees around the mouth of an exhausted horse. I told him not to stop because we were already close to Czyzewski's farm. This was a lie, but I did not want Moshe to give up.

We ran for another ten minutes, and the sky became lighter. In the distance, I saw a house. We dashed toward it. Czyzewski's! A large dog on a leash barked and lunged at us. The dog's master came out. He recognized us and restrained the animal. Carefully looking about, Czy-zewski opened the door of his barn and let us in. We collapsed and he closed the door.

VI

We slept all day. That night, Czyzewski brought bread and milk. "I came in several times earlier, but you seemed to be sleeping soundly, and I did not want to wake you." We were famished and ate greedily, mumbling our appreciation. "Stay quiet during the night," he warned.

After he left we wondered about Menucha, Yitzchak, Yerachmiel, mother, and Rachel and her family. None of my family knew we were there. We hid in a hole dug beneath the floor of the barn and covered by the floorboards, like at the widow's house. Again we had to lie on our backs face up with the sand and dirt sifting through the floor cracks onto our faces. We stayed there with few breaks.

The following day our host returned with potatoes, milk, and water, and placed it in the barn. He covered it with hay and told us where it was. "My wife and I are going away for the entire day to work in the fields. We'll return in the evening. Be quiet and don't let anyone learn that you are here." We did as he asked.

After dark, he ate dinner and came to the barn with bread. "Any news from Wegrow about the Jews there?" I asked.

"I was in the fields all day and didn't see or talk to anyone."

Days passed. From time to time, we heard sounds of artillery, but we didn't know whether it was German or Russian. It was now May 1943, and we ached to hear some good news. On a Sunday, Czyzewski told us he was going to church. We asked him to try to get some news about the Russian front and the Warsaw ghetto. When he left, we noticed that it was particularly quiet. We worried that other Poles would sneak around the barn listening for sounds. This was the usual way of learning things in these villages. Neighbors routinely eavesdropped, especially when Jews had prices on their heads.

Late in the afternoon, Czyzewski brought us some macaroni and milk. The Sunday meals were a bit better. He sat down with us. "The Russians are doing well and have surrounded the Germans along one section of the front. They captured some generals," he told us.

I asked about the Warsaw ghetto and Wegrow.

"In the Warsaw ghetto the Germans burned all the places where Jews resisted. All was destroyed. I have no news about Wegrow."

We took pleasure in hearing the news about the Russian front, but the news from Warsaw was depressing. A short time later Czyzewski learned that no Jews were known to be alive in Wegrow. I wondered if Rachel and her family were all right. It was unlikely that they were still at the Schultz's house. They might have gone to Potocki's, or they might have gone to Krip, about fifteen miles from Wegrow, where they had been hidden for the seven weeks after Yom Kippur. Isolated and anxious, we agonized, not knowing anything about the few people left in the world that we cared about. We did not know what to do.

We had to be careful not to ask Czyzewski too many questions, so as not to aggravate him. We listened carefully to what he volunteered on his own and never asked for more food or water or a better variety. We demanded nothing. We had to lie in our hole and be content. But our minds whirled constantly as the days passed without change.

Late one night, we left the hole to lie buried in the straw and fell asleep. In the morning we returned to the hole, careful to return everything just so, hoping Czyzewski would not find out. We had not seen him for a week. No one seemed to notice, so we stopped lying in the hole all the time. He came early, left food, and departed, not saying anything to us. On Sunday afternoon, however, he came into the barn and closed the door.

"How are you doing?"

"We are alive."

"I heard in church that on Saturday a Jewish butcher and his family were shot in a village where they had been hiding for a long time. Apparently someone had seen them and had informed the police."

We were very upset. This family had already suffered so much. They had not lived to see Hitler's end. We were afraid that Czyzewski himself might turn us in. But we had no alternatives.

I continued to wonder about Rachel, but I figured that she most likely had gone to Potocki. I decided to ask Czyzewski if he would take a letter to Potocki when he went shopping. Potocki had a store in Wegrow, where he sold blankets and comforters.

The following morning I left the hole early and waited in the straw for Czyzewski. When he came, I offered to pay him to take a letter to Potocki. He said he would have to talk it over with his wife. A few days later he agreed.

I was very pleased. I asked him for a pen, ink, and paper, and I wrote to Rachel in Yiddish, "Dear Rachel, I could not write you until now. I feel obligated to find out whether you, your mother, and your sister are alive. I cannot write you about our situation—you understand why—but I will try to help you in whatever way I can. You must know you can count on me. I would risk my life for you. When you have read this letter, write your own letter in reply and leave it with Potocki. Six days from now my host will take your letter back to me. I cannot write any more now. I end this letter with many kisses. Regards to all. Yours, Feivel." I addressed the letter "Rachel Mandelbaum" and dated it May 25, 1943.

I gave the letter to Czyzewski. "Don't deliver it or talk about it when strangers are around. Tell Potocki that you will return in six days to pick up the reply. If Potocki asks, tell him that someone met you in the forest and gave you the letter to deliver. Tell Potocki that he said he would harm you if you did not bring a reply in six days."

Czyzewski did as I asked. He returned and told me he was not asked about the sender and that the reply would be ready in six days. I was pleased. It indicated to me that Rachel was alive and staying with Potocki. I sagged with relief. At least I had something to think about and look forward to as I lay in that miserable hole in the barn. Rachel was alive!

I waited impatiently for that week to pass. We had heard no news from the front or about the rest of the family. We continued to hear artillery in the distance. After six days, Czyzewski told me he was going to Wegrow again. I reminded him to get the letter from Potocki when they were alone.

The day dragged. In the evening, Czyzewski came to the barn after eating supper and handed me the letter. He told me that Potocki again had asked no questions. There had been no conversation whatever between them.

I nervously opened the letter. Written in Yiddish, it read: "When I first got your letter, I could not read it. I was so overwhelmed to hear that you were alive that I could not continue. I didn't need to know anything else except that you were alive. After I calmed down, I was able to read the rest. I have been thinking of you constantly. I never lost hope that you were alive. My mother, sister, and I are living at Kreda's place. (I assumed Potocki had refused to let them stay with him.) There are some other people here also. It is very bad. Can you help me to get to where you are? My only wish is that we should be together, and that whatever happens to you will happen to me. I cannot tell you about everything. It is bad, and it would be terrible if I told you all. Whatever you do, it must be soon. I send you a thousand kisses. Yours, Rachel."

I read the letter over several times. I tried to read between the lines for any hint as to what she could not say outright. I gathered that she was afraid of being discovered, and when she referred to time being short, she must have meant that discovery was imminent. I had to do something as soon as possible.

What could I do? I wracked my brain for ideas but I couldn't come up with any. Where could I take her? Our hole was only big enough for two. In any case if I asked Czyzewski to take in anyone else, he would tell us all to leave. As it was, I felt he was not happy about being a courier. But I had suffered enough and I was going to move heaven and earth to save Rachel. She was right. Whatever happened would happen to both of us. Together.

VII

May in eastern Poland is a beautiful time of year. The air is resplendent with the fragrance of blossoms and freshly turned earth. Warm days are just around the corner, and the fragrances ride on pleasant spring breezes. It is a time of renewal, anticipation, and pleasant memories. But not if you are hiding in a hole in the floor of a barn wondering if your countrymen will come to kill you. I had to be with Rachel. It was only right. How many more spring days would we have together?

At the end of May, I wrote another letter and asked her to walk two miles outside Wegrow and meet me on the road to Jarnic by a large wooden cross. In the letter I directed her to sit on the grass behind the thorny flowers that surrounded the cross, so that she would not be seen from the road. Czyzewski's farm was eighteen miles from there, but we could get back to the barn by daylight. I would have to deal with Czyzewski then. I wasn't going to tell him that another person would be hiding in his barn.

Czyzewski wasn't going into town for ten days, because he thought visiting Wegrow too often would arouse suspicion. I wrote to Rachel expressing my appreciation for her letter and added: "On June 15, you should be at the place I am going to describe. There can be no deviation from this schedule. I have thought long and hard how I should meet you. You should go out at night along Garber Street, then along Live Street to the road to Jarnic. There, you will come across a large wooden cross surrounded by a flower bed, about three-and-a-half kilometers from Wegrow. Leave early enough so that you will arrive before midnight, and wait for me there. Make sure no one is watching or following you. I believe that if you follow these instructions, we will succeed in meeting. I wish you luck. Yours, Feivel."

I waited anxiously, and on June 7 I handed the letter to Czyzewski, asking him to deliver it by June 10 or not to deliver it at all. I thanked him profusely and wished him well on his journey.

That night I lay awake thinking of darling Rachel and how tolerable life would be when we were together again. The war would end. We could spend the rest of our lives together, maybe in Palestine. We could watch Shirley Temple on the screen—with Hebrew subtitles, not Polish. The nightmare would end. We would survive together.

Czyzewski left for Wegrow with his wife the next day, and I waited anxiously all day. In the evening they returned and ate supper. Then Czyzewski came to see us. He gave me back my letter. To it was attached a small note. "Rachel Mandelbaum and the others were shot on June 6!"

The color drained from my face. "What's the matter?" Czyzewski asked.

"A friend of mine died." He left. I read and reread the note. I learned after the war from Kreda's former bookkeeper that Rachel, her sister, her mother, and seven others had been hiding in Kreda's underground pit, the place that I urged him to construct. Someone had informed on them, and the SS came with two Polish policemen, took the ten Jews to a field outside town, and shot them. The bodies were tossed onto a truck two hours later and dumped into a pit at the Jewish cemetery.

If only I had convinced Czyzewski to go to Wegrow earlier, perhaps she would still be alive. Rachel! Rachel! Rachel! A beautiful woman, who had only lived to help others and make life pleasant, someone who filled a room with her smile. She had brought nothing but happiness to anyone who knew her. Lovely Rachel, who had never known the pleasure of being with a man.

I thought back to a conversation we had in April, when we heard about the Warsaw ghetto uprising.

"Let's get married now. Soon there will be no Jews left in Poland. Let's condense a lifetime of happiness into the few remaining days we have left."

"I understand how you feel, but let's not give up. We must continue to fight and claw to survive the war, to the last ounce of our strength. If we marry and you become pregnant, our situation will be even more hopeless. As it is, we have to save all our strength to run and hide in the dark and the cold and the rain, from forest to forest, without adequate food or shelter. What would happen if you were pregnant? You would have no doctor, no hospital, no bed, and no warm water. You might have to give birth in an open field in the dead of winter, with the howling wind and blowing snow, or in a dark, cold forest. You would bring a child into a world in which it was not welcome. And if, by some miracle, the child survived birth, how would you feed it? We can barely feed ourselves. If the baby gets hungry, it will cry, and we would surely be discovered and shot by our fellow Poles!"

"Are you still so naive to believe that we will survive this dark, filthy war? You are wrong! Live now, for shortly we will no longer be here on this earth. No one will even know what happened to us."

Rachel's words echoed over and over. She had been right. We would all die the same way, no one knowing where our bodies rested or what had happened. It would be as if we had never existed. We would not even be a memory in someone's mind. But why? I lay down and sobbed. I began to see visions.

"Shraga Feivel Bielawski! Descendant of the great rabbi, Shraga Feivel Danziger!"

"Who is it?"

"It is your great-great-great-grandfather."

"Rabbi Danziger. Is that you? What have you to tell me? Great rabbi, why is this happening to us? Why?"

"Feivele. My Feivele."

"Father, is that you, father? It is good to see you again. Can you tell me...."

"You. Jew from Wegrow."

"The ricksha driver from the Warsaw ghetto. I thought you were dead. How did you escape the Warsaw ghetto?"

"Uncle Feivel. It's me, Avram Mendele."

"Avram Mendele. You lived. The Lord God spared you, miracle child of my sister."

"Feivel, old friend. Can you see me?"

"Kreda? Kreda, I told you what would happen, if you did not take care. But you are alive? Here?"

"Shraga Feivel. Shraga Feivel. Feivel. Shra-a-a-ga Fei-ei-ei-vel."

"What? What is it? What do you all want? Why are you here? Have I dreamed the last four years? Was it a terrible nightmare?"

"Shra-a-a-ga Fei-ei-ei-vel. Shraga Feivel. Feivel."

"What is it?"

"Rachel Mandelbaum is dead."

"I know. I read."

"You will never see her again. She will not have your babies."

"I know."

Chapter 6

The Pit from Hell and the Angel Korczak

I

"Feivel. Feivel. You can't bring Rachel back. She is gone and you can no longer help her. If you destroy yourself, you will bring down the rest of the family with you. Mother will not survive. We all need you. So far you have helped to keep us all alive. We need you alive! Feivel. You haven't eaten in three days. Don't do this."

It was Moshe.

I heard, but I didn't care. The barn looked the same, but it didn't. The hay smelled the same, but it didn't. Nothing was the same. Nothing would ever be the same. Nothing made sense, and now I didn't care. What was the sense of hiding in a hole beneath the floor of a barn. So what if I lived? What then? What would the world hold for me? Moshe knew. He knew what I felt. He had lost Ethel.

But the Bielawski family lived on.

Why?

We just did, and, for some reason, that seemed to have its own logic. We just did.

Finally, I ate.

It was about this time, a week after the tragic news, that we noticed that our rations had shrunk. The food was being delivered every other day, instead of daily. I dared not complain. Czyzewski stopped talking to us. The pattern was familiar. He was having second thoughts, and any day he would tell us to leave. We just lay in our hole, covered by the boards, the sand sifting down on our faces.

At the end of June, Czyzewski came into the barn.

"You have to leave tonight. Immediately."

"Tonight? Give us some time to find out where we can go."

"No. Tonight. I'll return later."

We lay quietly pondering for about ten minutes and then decided to walk to Tofel's place, two and a half miles away in Jarnic. There, we hoped, mother, Yitzchak, and Yitzchak's family were hiding. Yitzchak and I had previously decided he would bring mother to Tofel's house if there were bad news from Wegrow. Late that night Czyzewski came back.

"Ready?"

"We'll leave about eleven o'clock. Leave the barn door unlocked and remove your dog. Thank you for hiding us. Tell your wife we said goodbye."

At eleven, we cautiously crept from the barn and headed for the forest. This was not the route to Jarnic, but we didn't want Czyzewski to know our destination. After about a half mile, we doubled back and found the way, an open road which invited trouble. We walked cautiously.

The gloomy blackness of pre-dawn night shrouded Tofel's house as we approached and knocked. After several minutes he got out of bed.

"Mr. Tofel. Over here. It's me. Shraga Feivel Bielawski."

"Bielawski? Eh? The younger brother?"

"Yes. We just came from the forest. We want to see our mother and brother. Please show me where they are."

"All right. Let me put some clothes on."

He took us to a corner of his field where the soil was sandy and too poor for growing crops. He left.

"Yitzchak. It's me, Feivel."

He emerged from the pit, then his wife and children.

"Feivel? Is that you? Feivel! I can't believe it. Look. Look who is here. It's Feivel and Moshe. They are still alive! Feivel. Look. See who is here with us."

It was Menucha. We were overjoyed, but we had to be quiet in the still night. Yitzchak told us that Yerachmiel and Itke had come from the forest also, but they could not remain in the hole because it was too small. It was clear that Tofel had not enlarged the pit as we had previously agreed and as I had paid him to do.

We had so much to talk about, but there was no time. It was late, and we had to decide where we would stay. Yitzchak said that Yerachmiel and his wife were lying in the fields among the tall stalks of growing rye. He suggested that we do the same. At night, when Tofel brought food, Yitzchak would talk to him and promise him an additional large sum of money if he would let us dig a larger hole so that we could all be together.

We decided to sleep in the fields and return the next night. We walked about a mile, and curled up in the cold, wet rye. In the morning we dozed while the voices of the farmers at work echoed in the distance. The morning sun dried the rye, and it was more comfortable. By noon, however, the heat became stifling and our throats were parched with thirst. It was unsafe to search for water until after dark.

When the stars had dotted the sky, we carefully returned, taking a roundabout approach. We watched from some distance to make sure no one was around. Then we crept to the hole and announced ourselves. Yitzchak stumbled out, greeted us, and offered some dried potatoes, which Tofel had put in the oven early and baked all day. Yitzchak handed us a can of water, too. We ate and drank greedily. Yitzchak told us that Tofel had agreed to allow us to expand the pit, but said he could not bring the tools and lumber for several days.

Before dawn we went back to the rye fields. We followed this routine for three days. On the second night, we met Yerachmiel and Itke, who had sneaked away from the fields to the pit, too. We had not seen them for over a year, and we hugged each other and celebrated.

Tofel finally brought the lumber and shovels. He had deliberately bought old lumber so that no one would notice new boards lying in the field. He had an extra treat, too. Our meal consisted of potatoes and water with a loaf of bread. We ate quickly so we could get to work.

We decided to dredge a new pit and not to make the hole as large as we had wanted. We had few boards and little time. The pit would be six feet square and four feet deep. All night we labored diligently, but could not finish, so we camouflaged the surface of the unfinished hole. I told Yitzchak to ask Tofel for a saw, and then Moshe and I returned to the field.

We heard the farmers laughing merrily and talking as they worked. They were happy. They were free. They feared no one, but we had to worry about everyone, even little children. We waited impatiently.

In the evening, we returned and wolfed down our food. The four brothers worked feverishly to complete the digging. Before dawn, the pit was ready. Excess soil was tossed away to avoid telltale traces of work. We covered all the boards with soil carefully, except for the twenty-by-twenty-four-inch board that served as a door. Then we edged the door with lumber and covered it with dirt and sod. Five fist-sized holes in the wood provided ventilation. We hoped that more grass would grow right above us as we were lying there, so our pit would have more camouflage. A fine grave, I thought.

By the time we finished, it was beginning to get light. We were ex-

hausted from long hours of digging and from lying six days in the rye
fields, so we all climbed into the pit and covered it. I fell into a deep
sleep.

The ten of us entered our new "home" on July 6, 1943. My mother,
Yitzchak, his wife Paula, their two children Renya, seven, and Eddie,
three, Yerachmiel, Itke, Menucha, Moshe, and me. For nearly four years
we had lived in fear, the men hiding most of the time. We had spent
much of our savings and had no decent clothes and few possessions. We
were living in a dirt pit in a field, and we were at the mercy of Tofel.
But we were alive. Few Jews from Wegrow had been that lucky. It was
a tight fit and we squeezed close together. The July heat weighed like a
steel anvil in those early days, and, at times, we felt woozy.

At noon that first day, we stirred and awoke. The heat struck us like
a blow to the head, and we stripped to our underwear, baking in silence
all day. At night, we scrambled through the door and gulped breaths
of fresh air before reentering. At eleven, I opened the door and poked
my head above the pit, inhaling the fresh air of the fields. It was wonderful. We all got out, the heat trailing behind us. We felt like loaves of
bread from the oven.

Tofel arrived with a pot of potatoes and a pitcher of water.

"Did you finish the pit?"

"Come. Here. Inspect it."

He checked over the boards, the door, and the pit. "Looks good to
me. I wouldn't know it was there, if you hadn't told me." He left satisfied
and we sat outside for the rest of the night, cooling off and allowing the
pit to air out.

At daybreak, we climbed back in and dozed until late morning. Then,
I asked Menucha to tell us about her escape. She removed the bandage
over her left shoulder revealing a hole just above her collarbone. I could
see all the way through! I felt sick just looking at it and fainted. Moshe
doused me with water and I came to. Menucha told her story.

"No one made it to the hiding place that Kreda had dug. The Germans
and Poles came in with their machine guns and ordered everyone out.
I slipped away, dived beneath a pile of old boards and covered myself,
lying still. I heard the others shouting and pleading for mercy, but they
shot everyone, including the children, and counted the dead. Seventeen
bodies. They went inside again and counted the nineteen names of the
workers on Kreda's list. Two were missing. After searching all over, the
Germans gave up and left. But one Polish policeman remained. He
muttered that he had to find the dog Jews. He began to remove boards
from the pile and found me. He dragged me through the street to an
open space where he pointed his gun at me. 'Don't you know me?' I
asked him. 'Let me go! No one is watching!' He refused. I was wearing
a silk nightgown. I tore out of his grasp and ran. He ran after me and

fired. I fell, bleeding, and he thought I was dead. He left. After a few minutes, I got up and ran toward the fields, bleeding profusely. I didn't stop until I came to a house with an open shed. I collapsed in the shed. Soon the owner came in. I recognized him—Czyzewski the tax collector. (He was not related to the man who had hidden us.) He saw me bleeding and became frightened. He wanted to know what had happened, and I told him."

"He asked what he could do to help. I told him to bring some warm water and clean clothes to wash the blood off. He returned in a few minutes and helped me wash up. I made a bandage of the cloth and covered the wound. The pain was excruciating, but I bit my lip and continued. There was nothing else to do. Czyzewski brought some milk and left."

"Later Czyzewski returned. I ate and redressed the wound. All the people at Kreda's had been shot except for two, Czyzewski said. One was Kreda's son, Yitzchak, who had not slept there that night, and the other was me. When they came to remove the bodies, mine was not there, Czyzewski related. He was afraid and told me I had to leave the shed before I was discovered. After dark, I left for Saszym's. On the way I came to a row of barns, and spotted Pierkowski in one of them. I decided to go there instead of Saszym's. As I approached and called him by name identifying myself, he yelled, 'Jesus! I thought you were shot! How did you get here?' 'Let me inside,' I said, 'and I'll tell you.' He told me to go up to the hayloft and lie there."

"He worked outside for another hour, then he came inside to ask if I wanted to see a doctor. I said no. Then he walked to the pharmacy and bought me some peroxide and cotton. He came with it and told me to hide in the hay."

Pierkowski was the bachelor who had the live-in housekeeper. He had been storing some of our valuables and could be trusted, but the woman was an anti-Semite and would surely turn Menucha in, if she knew of her presence.

Menucha stayed there for several days hiding in the hay and was almost lanced by the pitchfork once when the woman unknowingly jabbed the haystack as she was feeding the cattle. Finally, Pierkowski told her she would have to leave, and he offered to take her to Tofel's place.

Pierkowski had provided her with some clothes, and that night they left with him supporting her. She used a large stick as a crutch.

"He crossed himself and prayed for a safe journey. We walked through the fields and came to the Jewish cemetery, where he told me to find father's grave and ask him for a safe journey. I could not find it in the dark, so I chose another and prayed. We walked for four hours, and he left just before we reached Tofel's. I went up to the window and knocked. When Tofel came out and saw me, he nearly fainted. 'I thought you

had been shot,' he said. Seeing that I was not feeling well, he led me to
the pit where the family was. They were sitting outside to cool off, and
when they saw me, we all celebrated. They had given me up for dead."

By the time Menucha had finished telling us her story, it had become
very hot. The pit reeked of perspiration, and we were drenched with
our own sweat. We each had only a small piece of bread and some water
to last us all day. At midnight, two of us picked up the container of
potatoes and the pitcher of water at a prearranged place. When we
returned, everyone left the pit and breathed in the fresh cool air. I
looked up into the sky, and the stars seemed to revolve around and
around endlessly.

Toward morning we all returned to the pit, which was still warm from
the preceding day. I asked mother what had happened while she was
staying with the religious Catholic couple in Jarnic and how she had
come to Tofel's. She told her story.

"I had hidden beneath the floorboards of the couple's house. After
some time they allowed me to get out late at night and stay in the house.
In February we heard several shots coming from town. He closed the
door, left the house, and returned a few hours later. He told me that
another Jewish family, by the name of Kawer, had been in Jarnic for a
long time."

The family consisted of the mother, Chava, and her three sons Yaakov,
Yisroelke, and Mordechai. They were intelligent and wealthy people.
They had been involved in exporting grain from the Polish country
squires to Germany. Someone had found out that they were hiding in
Jarnic and had informed the Germans. They had all been shot. Mother
continued.

"Hearing this, I feared the same would happen to me. The man
said to me, 'Why are you so frightened? Why do you bother to hide?
You know that Jesus said that there would come a time when all the
Jews would be destroyed for the sin they committed. Now is that
time. Therefore you should not hide and plague yourself, running
from one hiding hole to another. You see that the time has come for
all Jews to disappear from the world. I tell you this because I pity
you for your troubles, but this is your fate. No one can change it.' I
was shaken by these words. 'Don't you know me as a decent person?
What harm have I done? Do I deserve to die?' He didn't answer. I
was afraid that he would betray me, but I had no alternative but to
remain there. My only hope was that Yitzchak would come to see me
and perhaps take me away."

"When Yitzchak came, I told him what he had said. I told him I did
not want to remain there. Yitzchak told the Pole he was taking me out
for some fresh air. He agreed, and we promptly left to go to Tofel's.
Since that time, we have been together."

The endless, stifling days dragged. Soon, when we went for the potatoes and water, we noticed that the food had not been washed. We could feel the sand and grit as we ate. After the heat of the long day, this was a difficult meal to eat, but this became our daily ration. Once or twice a week we received some bread and milk. How long could we take this?

I was curious to know what had transpired with Yerachmiel and Itke while I was still alive to hear, and so Yerachmiel told us his story.

"After the wedding, the Jewish police came and took us from our bed and sent us to Mord, a labor camp where we were assigned to shore up the bank of a river. Itke made friends with the Polish supervisor, and he gave her lighter work in his house. She cleaned, washed, and cooked for him. At night, she went back to the camp to sleep. This was the way we lived and worked until November. Then we heard that the Germans were taking all the Jews from Wegrow, Sokolow, Siedlce, and Kaluszyn and shipping them to Treblinka. We escaped into the forest, because there was no fence around the camp. We fled to a Pole's farm and paid him for hiding us there for a short time. A few days later the Pole told us that the Kreda family had been allowed to live and operate their laundry in Wegrow. I decided to go to see Kreda. I paid the Pole to take me there, because the trip would be risky, if I were alone. He loaded a wagon with hay, hid me and Itke in it, and took us to Kreda's. We were actually there the same time as you for a few hours, but we never knew that you were there too. Kreda told us we could not work there because the official list of workers was restricted. Itke was able to find a job making down comforters for a shop that sold them."

The owner of the shop was Potocki, the same Potocki who had acted as courier for my letters to Rachel. In return for making comforters, Potocki allowed Yerachmiel and Itke to stay in a back room and provided them with food and a place to sleep. They stayed there until June 1943. Then, afraid they would be discovered by the Germans, Potocki told them to leave.

"We left late at night and traveled without knowing where we were going. Near dawn we reached Liv. We saw a small isolated house in the distance, far from the neighboring houses. We knocked on the door and an older man came out. Itke recognized him because she had made some comforters for him. She asked him to let us come inside."

"She asked if we could stay during the day because it was dangerous for us. He thought for a moment, then told us to follow him to the barn. We hid for a week. Then we had to leave because he was afraid the Germans would find us. I thanked him, paid him for the time we had been there, and asked him how to get to Jarnic. We traveled in the dark forest, but got lost and had to hide. It took three days to find Tofel's place and the family."

II

For days we lay in our little underground oven like roasted animals. We prayed that the Germans would soon be defeated, but we heard no news from the Russian front. I recalled what the rabbi had taught us in Hebrew School when we were children. He had said that every Jew must perform good deeds, *mitzvos*, and that if he did he would go to the Garden of Eden after he died. If he did evil, he would go to *gehinom* (hell). He explained that hell was a great, hot oven. When I had heard this, I confess it did not make much of an impression on me. Under normal circumstances one has no conception of what it could really be like. But now, lying with nine other people in a narrow pit in the summer heat, I understood what hell was.

We pleaded with God to bring the night as quickly as possible so we could get out into the open air. As hungry as we were, we could barely eat the sandy potatoes and water that awaited us. Tofel could not buy us extra food in Wegrow without arousing suspicion. I asked him not to buy extra livestock or other expensive items for his house with the money we were paying him. His neighbors knew that his farm was not yielding much, and they would become suspicious in no time. He promised he would be careful.

When Tofel returned from church on Sunday, he reported to us that the Germans were retreating. He also told us that the underground Polish newspaper advised all Poles to notify the authorities of any Jews they knew about. He told us to be careful.

On August 3, 1943, Tofel said the Jews in Treblinka had staged an uprising the day before, burning the camp and killing many SS troops. We were pleased to hear it. Perhaps the Jews there knew that the war would soon end. We clung to that hope and encouraged each other. Somehow we dared to believe that we might actually outlive Hitler.

A few days later, Tofel came to us in the middle of the night with some bread, an unexpected treat. He told us he had been to Wegrow and bought the bread and two pigs for his sty. We were happy to have the bread, but I worried that he would arouse suspicion with his purchases. By now he had amassed a tidy sum of money, and he was eager to spend some. We thought and decided to give him a plausible alibi. I told him that if anyone should ask, he could tell them that his mother-in-law had loaned him money. He thought for a minute and said, "You are correct. People are very bad, and they kill for little reason. I hear it said that Polish youths are out searching for Jews in the fields and forests, killing them when they find any. They brag about how many Jews they have killed in the past several days. It is hard for me to listen to this, but there is nothing I can say. If I said anything against them, they would accuse me of supporting Jews and perhaps hiding them. This is a very bad time for Jews. From what I hear from my neighbors and friends, the Jews have no friends. I believe that I am the only friend they have."

We thanked him. To avoid the roving gangs, we stayed in the pit later at night, leaving less time to cool off. The food was even more stale than usual. But we had to take every precaution. We feared the Polish youths, even more than the Germans.

The next Sunday Tofel told us that upon leaving church that morning, one of his friends asked him for some matches. Tofel said he didn't have any, and his friend remarked, "You support a whole family of Jews at your place, and you don't have enough for matches?"

Tofel answered, "I don't know what you are talking about. Why do you suspect me? I don't know any Jews, and I don't have any at my place."

The man said, "It is so rumored in the village."

We told Tofel it was because of the pigs he had bought. He dismissed this idea and told us we had nothing to fear, but after he left we realized that such rumors would eventually lead Polish gangs to Tofel's farm. Once again, we needed a new hiding place, at least until the rumors died. Perhaps we could then come back. We drew lots, and Yitzchak and I were chosen to search.

At midnight, we crept through the rye fields, looking about aimlessly until we came to a farm house. After half an hour we thought we heard footsteps and lay in the field listening quietly. Two men carrying rifles on their shoulders passed. A half hour later, as we were continuing, we heard shots in the distance. Nervously, we walked until we reached the village of Zajacy.

In the distance, we saw houses of all sizes. We approached the smallest, most isolated one. In our hands, we clutched large sticks, ready to fight. I knocked as Yitzchak hid. After five minutes of knocking, a short man dressed in night clothes opened the door a crack. He was about five foot five, forty years old, with a long, wrinkled, tan face.

"What do you want?"

"I'm sorry for waking you. I'm from Wegrow and have been hiding in the forest. I had heard that the Germans are coming to search for us tomorrow. Could you hide us for a day or two until the danger passes."

He carefully studied me. "Does your family have a lumberyard?"

"Yes."

"I bought lumber for my house and barn from your father. I didn't have enough money to pay, but your father trusted me and extended me credit until I could pay. Your father was a fine man."

Yitzchak approached us slowly. "Who is he?"

"My brother."

"How many people altogether?"

"Six." I was afraid that he would be unwilling to hide ten.

"I'll have to consult with my wife."

She began to scream when he told her.

"What about your two small children? They will be left alone, if something happens to us."

"These are good people, and good people should be helped in times of trouble. It is a matter of saving innocent lives, and it will only be for two days."

"No. No. It is too dangerous."

"Their father was good to us. No one else had been willing to lend me any money." Finally she became quiet. "What do you say?"

"Let them come."

The farmer's name was Edward Korczak, and his wife was Marta. Marta was a plain woman, who stood about the same height as her husband, wore a handkerchief around her hair, and worked hard to keep her children neatly dressed and the house clean. Korczak told me to act swiftly and bring the family before daylight. He pointed to a ladder standing near the house and said that when we came back we should climb up to the loft and hide in the hay. We thanked him and left quickly.

While going back for the others, we thought about what to do with the four people we had not told him about. We decided that two children and two adults would sneak up while he was not looking.

When we reached the pit, we could hear crying from inside. We knocked on the boards. They were ecstatic to see that we were still alive. They had heard some shooting and assumed that we were dead. They were sure that they, too, would die, having nowhere else to go. The Polish thugs would eventually find and kill them, too.

We told them we had a place to go and advised them to hurry so we could get there while it was still dark. We wanted to make sure Korczak would not know there were ten. At dawn, we arrived and two of us quietly climbed to the attic. Then more followed with the children. By the time Korczak came out, only six of us were visible. The others were hidden in the hay.

III

Although we were stuffed into the hay of Korczak's loft, our new accommodations seemed luxurious. We experienced the freshness and open air of daytime for the first time in an eternity and fell into deep, contented sleep, oblivious to the world. Later, Korczak came and said, "I told our two children some people were hidden in the attic because the Germans would kill them if they found them. I told them to keep it a secret and not mention this to their playmates or anyone else, because their father and mother would also be killed, if the Germans knew. They promised not to tell." The children were six and seven.

He had killed a goose for us. "Will two of the women come down to the kitchen and cook it? I'll supply flour, milk, butter, eggs, and bread."

"We would rather not. The neighbors might see us."

"My wife is not familiar with city cooking. I will close the curtains so no one can look in. Don't worry. No one comes to my house anyway."

Paula and Menucha went down, and Marta was more than cooperative. They asked for flour and eggs and kneaded the dough for noodles. They washed the goose thoroughly and cut it up into a large pot adding parsley and carrots before cooking, just as they had at home.

Marta kept the door closed. She was interested in seeing how the cooking was done, and watched carefully. Then they brought the food up to us. It was incredibly delicious! We could not recall ever having eaten a more wonderful meal. It was as if we were home again.

After dinner, we thought about what was happening. Was all this a dream? Was Korczak an angel in the guise of a man? We couldn't understand it. Perhaps, he knew that the war would soon end and figured it would be useful to be kind to us. Nevertheless, we had not been treated like this before, and it made little sense to us.

Then the answer came. There were some Poles who cared and acted bravely, as kind, feeling, decent human beings. Not everyone turned his back on the Jews. And after ten years, my father had reached out to us from the grave. His acts of charity had provided us with a haven. Goodwill and human understanding stretches on and on and is sometimes repaid under the strangest circumstances! We fell asleep contented.

When we awoke, there was Korczak with some fresh bread, butter, and milk. We hadn't had fresh bread and butter for a long time. What was going on? Were we crazy or was Korczak?

"I went to the village and heard that the Russians are defeating the Germans all along the front."

"How much do I owe you for all this?"

"I'll figure it out, but I don't want to make any profit from you."

"We do not expect you to work for us for nothing."

"I don't want to take anything from people who once had everything and lost it all."

We looked at each other in disbelief.

In the evening we covered ourselves with hay and slept well. Korczak came the next morning. "Have two women come down to cook. Do you want another goose?"

"No, the neighbors will notice the geese missing." We also didn't know how long we would stay there and didn't want to use up the available food. "Do you have milk and flour?"

"You are welcome to it."

Menucha and Paula again went down in the kitchen, closed the curtains and door, and cooked macaroni and fresh milk. They brought it up to us, and it was delicious. We gobbled it down.

Korczak later delivered a newspaper from the village. We had not seen one in six months.

"Could we go down to wash ourselves one at a time? We have not bathed in six weeks."

"Yes, but do you want anything to eat first?"

"Anything you have will be fine."

While we waited, we each took a section of the paper and read it thoroughly, looking particularly for news from the front, but, as we expected, there was none. The press was censored by the Germans.

Korczak came back with fresh bread, eggs, butter, and milk. After the meal we went down one at a time to wash. Six of us washed that day. By now, Korczak knew that there were ten, but he was willing to let us all stay indefinitely. We again read the newspaper, trying to find something by reading between the lines.

We slept well in the fresh air and ate well the next day. He slaughtered two hens for the women to prepare and they served the chicken with potatoes and gravy. The remaining four of us washed in the meantime. The meal was delicious and we felt human again.

So it went. Each day we had good food. On Saturday, Korczak asked us how we were. He told us he had a neighbor who lived about 300 feet away and warned us that he was an anti-Semite. He had three children, ages six, seven, and nine, who played together on the weekend. He advised us to be very quiet so that the children would not hear us as they were playing in the yard next door. He told us he would slaughter another goose for us on Sunday.

We were convinced that he was indeed an angel sent to save us. We figured we could survive the war staying right here in Korczak's attic. On Sunday the Korczaks went to church. His children remained behind to play with the neighbor kids. They jumped, laughed, and jostled each other. Some climbed the corner of the house as they played. These farmhouses were built of heavy lumber, each about four inches tall and twelve inches wide. The corners of the boards overlapped in log cabin fashion, so each beam protruded about one foot. The children were easily able to climb up on these protrusions.

As we peered out of the hay to see what they were doing, we saw one of the neighbor's children looking into the attic. He immediately climbed down. We thought he had seen one of us! We assumed he was running home to tell his father. We were sick. We were painfully aware that we would have to leave!

When Korczak returned, he brought news of Russian victories, but his happiness faded when we told him what had happened and said we didn't want to place him in any danger. We proposed that we go into the forest for a few days until it was certain that no one knew about us. If all remained quiet, we would return. He agreed. Korczak told us that if we were ever hungry, we could come back and he would bake bread for us.

It pained us deeply to have to leave this ideal setup after such a short time. We knew we would never find another like it. At midnight, Paula and I went down to look for another hiding place. We had no particular destination in mind, but we walked on and came to a house about a mile away. The door was open, and a light was on inside. We could see a man and a woman standing near an oven. He was moderately tall with straight blond hair and a large build. He had a healthy-appearing full, red face. The woman was attractive and of medium build.

No sooner had their dog begun to bark than the man came out and spotted us. He looked like a typical Polish farmer. He asked what we wanted and we received permission to come inside. We gave him the routine about hiding in the forest.

"I know you." Apparently, he had bought lumber from us.

"Could you hide us for a week? We'll pay you in gold."

"I don't know. I have a still for making vodka and the Germans might come here to check on me. If they find you, my family and I would be in danger. Besides, I have no room in the house."

"We could dig a pit in the field."

"The ground is shallow. You will hit water."

"We can dig the hole in such a way that this would not be a problem. We have ten people."

He wanted an exorbitant amount of money. I took Paula aside and discussed this with her. We had no other choice and decided to accept his conditions.

"I really don't want you here and that is why the price is so high. I didn't think you had that much." He went to ask his wife, Halina, and told her it was a large sum of money and that we were honest people. She left it up to him.

"Bring your family. My name is Waclaw Bujalski. My wife's name is Halina and I have two children, five and six." He led us to a large brick-walled barn some distance from the house and showed us a ladder. "Go up into the attic of the barn when you come back. I will leave the barn door open. Be quiet because my brother lives nearby and will inform the Germans, if he finds out.

We assured him we would be very quiet. We left and returned to the rest of the family about two o'clock. We hurried them along in order to travel the mile quickly.

When we reached the barn, we climbed into the loft. It was a very long barn, about 100 feet. The attic floor was solid except for the large opening through which we climbed. It was nearly full of hay. After settling in I told the family how we had negotiated for the place and the amount of gold I had promised him. By this time, we were all tired and soon fell asleep.

In the morning Bujalski came into the barn and called his pigs for feeding. Then he came up, and I introduced the family. He gave us bread and milk, saying that he didn't have time to prepare anything more. He said he was going out to work in the fields and would return near evening. He removed the ladder that we had used to climb up.

We ate and enjoyed the food. The air in the barn was good and fresh. I looked down and saw several cows at the trough. There were some pigs, a horse, ducks, geese, and chickens. Late in the day, Bujalski came back and led the horse and the cows to the trough. Then he called to the pigs for feeding. This was his signal for our feeding also. He gave us potatoes, bread, and milk. He was tired from working all day and didn't speak much. We ate, breathed the fresh air, and fell asleep.

The same routine was repeated the next day. His wife came out with him to milk the cows. He told us that on Tuesday, market day, he was going to Wegrow to sell his homemade vodka. He said he would buy bread for us then. He shooed the animals into the field, and he and Halina left to go to work.

I looked out of the hole provided for ventilation, which was about the size of a fist, and saw the farmers in the distance working their fields. The sun was shining and it was warm. I saw the cat sitting on the porch of the house sunning itself. I envied its comfortable, carefree existence. We had to worry about what the future had in store for us, but the cat could doze in the sun. The day passed slowly, and we fell asleep early.

In the morning Bujalski brought us macaroni and milk.

"Bring us some news about the war," I asked.

He returned in the evening and came to see us after having eaten supper. He brought us potatoes with sour cream and milk. "The war is going well and will soon end." He had bought bread for us in Wegrow because he was afraid to let his wife do too much baking. The neighbors would see smoke rising from his chimney and might suspect he was having to do extra baking to feed some Jews.

The next few days passed in the same manner. On Sunday he heard that several Jews had appeared in Jarnic on Saturday asking for bread. They had been discovered and shot by members of the Polish underground.

It had now been a week since we arrived, and I asked Bujalski if we could stay for another month. He was willing to keep us, but he was afraid we would be discovered in the hayloft. He had no other hiding place. I said we would dig a hole in the field, if he would supply the tools.

A few days later he told us he had the tools and boards and we could come down to start digging. He led us to a spot in the rye field and reminded us that it had to be a shallow hole because of the high water table. In the dark of night, we dug the dirt and removed it. It took all night.

We returned to the barn before light and spent the day there. That night we all went to the pit. We entered this new hiding place on September 1, 1943, exactly four years to the day after the Germans had invaded Poland.

The pit was shallow, damp, and hot. We had to sit close to one another. As we had done at Tofel's place, we sat in our underwear because of the heat. Small holes in the boards covering the pit provided ventilation. It was inadequate for ten people.

Late at night Bujalski brought us food and water. He demanded payment for the entire month. We didn't want him to know that we were carrying money with us, so we told him we would have to go to the forest that night to dig some up where we had hidden it.

The next morning he brought us soup, bread, and potatoes, and I paid him a month's rent in gold dollars. He was satisfied. We ate the soup and saved the bread for later. During the day it was too hot to eat. We waited for night to go out for some fresh air. We savored each breath, knowing we would have to return to the stifling conditions of the pit as soon as it began to get light.

The following week Bujalski began harvesting the rye in his fields. He made sheaves, putting ten sheaves into one bundle so they could stand and dry in the sun. He had no time to make moonshine and had no reason to go to Wegrow. He therefore did not buy bread that week, and we had less to eat.

At the start of our third week, it was unusually hot and humid. The air was heavy, and it became hazy and cloudy. Soon we heard thunder, and it began to pour in torrents. A trickle of water entered the pit, then a steady stream. We didn't know what to do. If we left the pit, the neighbor would see us. If we remained in the pit, we would drown!

Bujalski came to see us in the early afternoon and asked about our situation. I pleaded with him to do something before we drowned. He quickly ran and placed bundles of rye around the pit so we could sit on the edge of the hole and lean against the bundles without being seen. At nightfall we could sneak up to the attic of the barn, he told us. He left.

The children and mother got out first, then the other women and the men. Before I could get out, the walls of the pit collapsed, burying me in mud up to my waist. Moshe and Yitzchak had to pull me out. We sat next to the bundles of rye in our underwear in the drenching rain. We were cold and wet, and mother and the children shivered. We sat as close to one another as possible.

When night arrived, it was still raining. We ran across the field to the attic and went up, dripping wet. We thanked God that we had not drowned in the pit. At least we had a place to stay for the moment. In the hay, we warmed ourselves. In the morning, Bujalski left warm food and bread. We ate ravenously.

IV

A few days later Bujalski told us he was afraid to keep us any longer. Each farmer was required to give a percentage of his produce to the Germans, and he had not done so. He was afraid the Germans would come to collect their taxes, search his farm, and discover us. I asked him to give us a few days to find a new hiding place, and he consented.

We thought about returning to Korczak's place, but we would be in constant danger of being seen in the open attic. The next time we might not be lucky enough to escape.

I looked around and an idea came to me. I could build a false wall in the attic, much as I had done in our old house. The barn had been built relatively recently. The inside was plastered and the roof was thatched. The ceiling (the floor of the attic) was fourteen feet high and supported by large beams, eight inches square, which spanned the width of the barn at six-foot intervals. The floor of the attic consisted of flat boards, twelve inches wide and one and a quarter inches thick, suspended between the beams. These boards were in two layers. The boards of the first layer were about eight inches apart, and the second layer overlapped the first, covering the open spaces.

I figured I could build the false wall resting on the first beam, six feet from the end of the barn, and plaster it so it looked like the original end of the barn. As an entrance to this space, I would leave two of the flat boards unnailed, supported loosely by the beams. If one of us wanted to enter the enclosed area, he could place the ladder underneath, lift up the loose boards, and go up, using the entrance as a trap door. The two boards would be repositioned, and no one would be able to recognize that there was an opening at all. It would look from below just like the rest of the ceiling.

I told my plan to the others, and they thought it would work. But I still had to convince Bujalski. He would have to agree and supply the materials.

That Sunday we waited patiently for Waclaw and Halina to return from church. After eating, Yitzchak and I took him off to one side and told him we had a plan for a foolproof hiding place.

"Can this be done?"

"It can. I tell you what. I'll offer you a challenge. Because you and your wife are so afraid of our being discovered, I will build it and hide my family in it. I will then let you and your wife search for us. If you can find us, we will leave. But if you can't, you must allow us to stay indefinitely. Explain this to your wife. If you both agree, I will tell you what materials I will need to build it."

He agreed. An hour later, he returned to say they had accepted our bargain. I told him I would need lumber, a saw, a hammer, nails, plaster, sand, water, and a trowel. He would have to leave these materials in the barn, and we would take care of the rest. I also needed to know when I would be able to hammer so that his brother would not hear us. Once the work began, he could not come in until we had finished. He said he could have the materials together in two days and would think about what to do about his brother. He left satisfied.

The air was fresh, and we slept well. A few days later, he learned that his brother was going to Wegrow the following day, and we could start working then.

We brought everything up and waited for the word from Bujalski to begin. The next morning he brought us a pot of potatoes and some milk and told us his brother and his wife were definitely going to Wegrow, and that we would be able to start in a few hours. I reminded him that he could not come up to the attic until the work was done.

I began by measuring off six feet from the end wall and drawing a line there. My brothers cut the boards to size, and we started to build the false wall. We worked all day, and by evening, we had completed the false sidewall. When Bujalski came in with some bread, I told him I no longer needed to do any hammering, but we would still need three more days to finish the job. I would let him know when everything was finished.

The next day I began to plaster. I completed a small section to see if the color would match the opposite wall. The new plaster was lighter than the old, so I mixed some dust in with the paste until I succeeded in matching the shade. It took three days. I then cut two boards off the ceiling to serve as our secret entrance. From below no one could recognize this as a door, because the cut ends of the boards were hidden by the beams.

We then brought the ladder over, lifted up the two boards, and everyone got into the hiding place. I returned the ladder to its former place and waited for Bujalski.

When he came in with food in the evening, I walked over to him and took the food. "The place is finished. Everybody is in it. Come up and see if you can find them. Remember our agreement. If you find them, we will leave, and if you don't, we stay." He nodded.

He went up and looked everywhere, poking into the hay to be sure he hadn't missed anything. He could find nothing.

"It is impossible that anyone is hidden there. They must have gone elsewhere."

I teased him, but assured him they were all in the barn. "Call your wife and ask her to help search. She is more fearful than you about our being discovered. Perhaps she will do better. Let her find the nine people who are hidden here!"

He left and returned with Halina. A tall, thin, good-looking woman, who wore no makeup but still had rosy cheeks, Halina had few diversions in her life. This searching for the hidden guests was something of a game to her, and she delighted in turning the barn upside down looking for us. She looked everywhere, but she, too, could find no one. She went down to see if anyone was hidden below, again finding nothing. She told her husband, "They have all left. No one is here!"

I asked her if she were certain. She said she was. "If you are certain, then you must also be convinced that no stranger could possibly find anyone here. Is that correct? If I show you where my family is, will you agree to allow us to remain?"

"If you show me they are here, you may all stay."

I took the ladder from the open end of the attic and placed it against the opposite wall. I went up and knocked on the ceiling. My brother lifted the two boards, and I asked Halina Bujalski to climb the ladder. She saw the nine people lying on the floor and was dumbfounded!" "I am certain now that you will not be discovered. You may stay as long as you like."

I thanked her very much. I went up to join my family in the hiding place.

Chapter 7

Bujalski's Barn

I

By the time we had completed our new annex and convinced Bujalski that it was safe to keep hiding us, the chill of October was in the air and the leaves on the trees had begun to fall. The year 1943 had nearly ended, and we could now wait to see Hitler's grip on Europe end. As the temperatures dropped at night, we were thankful that we had brought coats with us, and that the warmth of the animals in the barn below us kept the loft reasonably comfortable.

Bujalski brought us food that evening, and we could tell by his manner that he had relaxed and accepted the new arrangement. Before we had built this hiding place, he had rarely spoken to us. Halina never brought the food. Now, both visited and talked freely with us. And there was a new respect. Bujalski could see that we were not only honest, but also clever and resourceful.

On Sunday afternoons, he spent long hours in the loft telling us what he had heard in church and in the village. He reported to us mainly news about the war and about the Jews. Although the Russians were doing better, it still appeared that the war would drag on. He had heard that the authorities kept good records. They had a good idea which Jews had been shipped to Treblinka, which had been shot, and which had gone into hiding. Bujalski had also heard that a band of young Poles had discovered a family of Jewish butchers hiding in the Jarnicer forest and had shot them. Later, the boys bragged about the terrific job they had done. Bujalski had known the family because they used to come to the village to buy cattle, and sometimes he had sold to them. He said it was a pity.

We believed that Bujalski was basically an honest person, though at times somewhat naive. If I spoke in simple, straightforward terms to him, he would believe almost anything I told him. The more he spoke with us, the more he trusted and believed us. Nevertheless, we worried that he might be influenced by the hate all around him and eventually betray us.

Our rations during this time were becoming more meager. Halina worked in the fields all day and was too tired to cook at night. Bujalski was still afraid to bake bread, and he traveled to Wegrow less frequently, to avoid arousing suspicion. Because it was autumn, he also had to harvest the grain in his fields and had no time to make moonshine, so he had even less reason to go to town. He brought us a five-pound loaf of bread every other day, which amounted to about a quarter pound per day for each of us. We would divide the bread into ten portions and make it last two days. On Sundays, he brought macaroni and milk.

My mother's health slipped, and she looked weak. She never ate her full portion of bread, but instead saved some for Yitzchak's little boy, Eddie. When no one was looking, she would give him the extra piece. He was a clever child, bright enough to realize that it was dangerous for him to cry. He was very quiet, never crying even when he was hungry. Although he was three and a half years old, he looked like a one-year-old, the poor diet having stunted his growth. His hands and fingers were as small as a baby's. Even with the extra bread, he was not getting enough nutrition.

He would sit next to his grandmother, and she would tell him stories about how it would be when the war was over. She told him he would have noodles with gravy, goose meat, fried hens, fresh cooked carrots, butter, fried eggs, cheese, challahs, kichel, cookies, strudel, cheese cake, honey cake, baked apples, pears, plum pudding, and all the delicious things we had once enjoyed. Eddie would salivate for hours. He would ask, "When will this be?" She would answer, "The time will come."

We were all hungry, but we could not complain. Worst of all was not knowing how long the tedium and hunger would last. It had been a year since we had become full-time fugitives, hiding from both the Poles and Germans, and over four years since the Nazi invasion.

One Sunday after church, Waclaw told us that he would need to take on an extra worker until the harvesting was completed. We were not happy, knowing that a stranger added new perils. Bujalski also realized this and asked if one of us could help him cut hay for his horse, so that no worker would need to come into the barn very often. I agreed, and he showed me a machine which shredded straw. Essentially, it consisted of a wheel attached to two blades. By turning the handle on the wheel, the operator could rotate the blades and slice the straw. He locked the barn door so no one could come in unexpectedly, and he put some straw in the shredder. I turned the wheel, but after a short time I felt dizzy. I became weak and collapsed, nearly unconscious. I heard him laugh, and then I passed out. I had been too weak to even turn the handle on a shredder.

I awoke, and regained my senses. I knocked on the ceiling, my brother lifted up the two boards, and I went up. They asked me if I had shredded a lot of straw. I told them what had happened, and they said they had had no idea that I was lying on the ground all that time. I rested and wondered for the ten thousandth time why it was that we had to suffer so.

Later that night, Bujalski came up and laughed as he described how I had fallen unconscious turning the shredder a few times. He looked at us, shook his head, and said, "I don't know why you try so hard to stay alive."

I wondered, too. But I knew. The world would learn of this. I owed that much to Rachel and all the others. At the same time, I desperately wanted to leave some testament that there were once Jews in Poland. I thought perhaps I could carve something out of wood.

Late at night I climbed down and searched for a suitable block of wood. Near the house, I found some thick pieces of firewood, birch wood. I took several pieces up to the hiding place with me. With a small stone that Bujalski brought, I sharpened my penknife and whittled.

First I carved into the wood a picture of the barn. In Hebrew I etched the words, "In this place we sat while Hitler murdered the Jews." On the back I carved my name and the date. Then I decided to replicate my father's tombstone. I wanted it to be known that we had descended from rabbis. Should any Jew survive the war, I hoped that he would find the carvings and observe my father's *yahrtzeit* (anniversary of his death). When this was completed, I carved Rachel's name and the date she was murdered by the Germans.

The carving took a long time, but it filled my waking hours and took my mind off the hunger. I showed the carvings to Bujalski and explained what they were. "If anything happens to us and if you should survive the war, contact any surviving Jew in Poland or elsewhere and tell him you have some interesting carvings. I'm sure you will be rewarded. I will hide them in a place where I know you will find them, if you just look around." He promised he would honor the request. But he never had to. And I still have those carvings with me today.

By the end of November, we realized we were slowly starving. A pitiful sight, Eddie was constantly hungry, despite the extra piece of bread. Only my mother's tales of the sumptuous meals that awaited him after the war kept him from giving up.

Moshe and I decided, without Bujalski's knowledge, to go to Korczak and ask him for food. Late at night, we stole from the barn and walked to Korczak's house, where we knocked on his door. We told him we were hiding in the forest, but did not have enough to eat. He looked at his rations and said he could spare us one five-pound loaf of bread. After I paid him, he thanked us and told us he thought of us often. He assumed that we were no longer alive. We thanked him and made our way carefully back to the hiding place.

On a Sunday about this same time, toward the end of November, Bujalski asked me and Yitzchak to join him in the barn below the loft. He looked nervous and said he wanted to chat. "The priest in church spoke from the pulpit today about the Jews. He told us, 'Jesus came from the Jews and was the Messiah. But the Jews did not believe in him and sentenced him to death, hanging him on a cross. Before they crucified him, Jesus said, "There will come a time that these people who will have spilled my blood will have their own blood spilled." Now you see that Jesus was correct, and what he predicted 2,000 years ago is now coming true. God himself does not come down from heaven, so he created a person by the name of Hitler who carries out what Jesus foretold. I feel sorry for these people, but this is the fate of the Jews. Now you can see with your own eyes that our God is the true God.' "

I felt a gnawing in my stomach. Bujalski continued, "My wife and I discussed this and have decided to ask you three questions. First, why do the Jews not believe in Jesus? Second, is it true that the Jews crucified our God? Third, why is Hitler such an enemy of the Jews?"

I sighed deeply. "I'll answer your questions the next time you come, because it would take too long to answer them now."

"That's fine with me. I'll see you again. Goodbye."

This worried us. Bujalski was a simple, honest man, but conflicting attitudes confused him. He was Catholic and attended church regularly. The priest explained why the Jews were being punished and, in essence, justified the actions of the Nazis. As a good Catholic he would be inclined to believe the priest. The Polish underground urged that the Jews be hunted, though the underground was supposed to be the Germans' enemies and the flame of Polish nationalism. The neighbors eagerly pursued the few Jews who were left in hiding. Only the Bielawski family and Bujalski's conscience told him he was doing the right thing in hiding us. We had to make certain he understood that the destruction of a race of people was the most heinous act ever perpetrated in the modern world. Our lives depended upon how we answered his three questions. It was time for me to assume a new profession—philosopher.

A few weeks later, on a Sunday in early December, Bujalski came up. "Any news?"

"I hear the Russians are pushing the Germans back, and many Germans are freezing to death deep in Russia. Their tanks and trucks are stuck, and they are leaving them behind to flee on foot. The Russians have captured an entire division and several high-ranking officers. The Poles believe the war will not last much longer."

"Heard anything about the Jews?"

"No. Most everyone says there are no Jews left."

"Do you have any time to spare right now?"

"Sure."

"Would it be all right if Yitzchak and I come down to speak with you about the questions you asked?"

"Yes."

We sat near him, and I began, "You wanted to know why we don't believe in Jesus. In the last year of Jesus' life, the Romans ruled over the Jewish land and the Jews. The Jews were required to obey their laws. Jesus was a wise man. He preached that he was the Messiah. However, the Jews did not accept him as the Messiah because the original Hebrew bible said that the Messiah would come at a time when the entire world was at peace, without war, and all people would be as brothers and sisters. At that time there was no peace. The Romans were waging wars against many peoples. It was for this reason that the Jews did not accept him as the Messiah."

"The Romans, however, watched Jesus closely. They saw him preaching to many people and gathering many followers. They were afraid that because he was wise, he might organize a revolt against the Romans. They therefore imprisoned Jesus and tried him as a revolutionary, sentencing him to death by crucifixion, the customary form of Roman execution. The Jews did not take part in his crucifixion."

Bujalski listened carefully to every word. Having heard me out, he said he was glad we had clarified these two questions. "I didn't know the Romans had crucified Jesus," he said. "I now have a better understanding. I have to go now, but next time I see you, you can answer my third question. Good night."

"Don't speak to any neighbors or friends about this. It might arouse their suspicion."

"I understand. I won't. Goodbye."

Yitzchak and I analyzed our interaction with Bujalski. We both thought that he had listened intently to every word and had seemed satisfied with our answers. We were relieved, but we still had to come up with a good answer to his third question for the next Sunday.

The next morning, Bujalski brought us bread and milk, greeting us with a smile and a cheery "good morning." He was in a good mood. We hoped it was because he was beginning to understand the differences between Jews and Christians in a positive way.

That week was a good one. He began to feed us better. We weren't sure whether it was because of our answers or because the Russians were faring well against the Germans. Perhaps, he was beginning to feel that he was doing the right thing in hiding us.

The next Sunday we saw Bujalski and his wife ride off to church. We hoped he would bring us good news. In the afternoon he returned in an extremely buoyant mood.

"The Germans are losing on all fronts. They have become more ruthless. They now enter villages where farmers have not paid taxes, shoot their hogs and cows, and take the carcasses with them. A friend told me there are still Jews hiding in the forest and that they should be killed, so that there will be no witnesses after the war. Be very careful."

"We will. You may be sure of that. Do you have time to hear our answer to your question as to why Hitler hates the Jews so?"

"Yes. Certainly. I would like to hear that very much."

"When Hitler wanted to take power in Germany, there was a recession in Germany. Many Germans had no work. Hitler was a good orator. He figured that to be successful he would have to find a scapegoat for the bad economic situation. He found it easy to blame the Jews. He said the Jews were the wealthiest people in Germany. They owned the banks, factories, businesses, and the nicest homes. They were good lawyers, physicians, and engineers. Because the Jews were so greedy, he said, they underpriced German businessmen and drove them out of business. Jewish engineers were taking credit for new discoveries. Jewish lawyers were winning most of their cases. Jewish doctors were better than German doctors and taking up all the new patients. Germans were not able to compete and were falling behind economically."

"Hitler proposed a plan to bring prosperity back to Germany so that all Germans would have work and Germany would become stronger than any other country in Europe. First, everything that the Jews owned would be taken from them and divided among the Germans. The jobs that the Jews held would be given to the Germans. His plan for accomplishing this was secret, and he would disclose it only after he was elected chancellor of Germany."

"In addition to using the Jews as scapegoats to achieve his political ambitions, Hitler also believed that the German people were the true master race, the superior Aryan race. He did not want the blood of Jews intermingled with Aryan blood. In Germany many Jews had already become very assimilated and had married Germans. He could not stand to see this 'poisoning' of Aryan blood, and so he determined to destroy all the Jews."

Bujalski nodded his head and said, "The answers to these questions are very important to me. I would never have known why the Germans hated the Jews so much."

I then explained that this was not a war between the Germans and the Jews, but one between the Germans and the rest of Europe. "Now you can see that what Hitler had promised the German people before he came to power, a solution to the Jewish problem, has in fact come true. The Germans are pleased with him and are waiting for the day when they will be the pure Aryan race, superior to all other people on earth. They started with the Jews because they are a minority against whom they would have much support. But if the Germans win the war, they will then enslave the Poles. If the Poles had understood this, they would have joined with the Jews and organized an effective stand against the Germans. The war could now be over. Instead, the Germans have divided their enemies. The Poles have killed many Jews, their potential allies, and all of Europe is still in danger."

Bujalski was by now red-faced and perspiring over what he had heard. He was very excited. "Now I understand that you are correct. I believe that the Jews would have fought to the last drop of blood, because they had nothing to lose. It is very late. Good night." Again I pleaded with him not to discuss this with anyone else.

It occurred to me later that the Jews had no guns, no weapons, no way to fight the Nazis—except the bullets I had just fired. If only I had been able to sit down with every Pole in the country and tell him this. If only I could explain why the Jews were not their enemies and why the ancient religious hatreds were based on ignorance and misunderstanding. True Christians would never believe that humans must be destroyed, just as no Jew would believe this. Bujalski inherently understood this. He just needed to have someone explain it to him in clear terms.

Where had the Jews failed? By not trying more forcefully to explain all this to their fellow countrymen years before. Maybe the Poles would not have listened. But we should have tried. It isn't enough to live side by side with people and tolerate their prejudices. They must be told how their prejudices are hurting themselves and others, even if most won't listen. Hitler didn't kill the Jews. Ignorance and fear killed them, and it took Bujalski's questions to make this clear. Never again, never again, never again should people be allowed to pass on their hate from generation to generation. It was everyone's responsibility to see to this, not just the Jews' responsibility.

II

Just before Christmas, Bujalski and Halina traveled to Wegrow to shop. He brought back some bread and more good news about the progress of the war.

"I would like all of you to come into the house for a Christmas Eve dinner."

"That would be wonderful! But we might be seen by the neighbors."

"Don't worry. You could come at midnight. The doors and windows will be locked and the curtains drawn."

"Will we be able to wash up before dinner?"

"Yes. Come down one at a time."

"Thank you. That is quite generous of you."

After he left, we talked about how nice his invitation was. We waited impatiently for Christmas.

But as the time for the dinner approached, we became nervous. What if this generous gesture backfired, and we were spotted by a neighbor and turned in? To be caught just as the Germans appeared to be on the run! But we were so hungry, we took the chance.

Before midnight, he summoned us and we followed him inside the house. It was the first time we had been in Bujalski's home. The rooms were spacious, and our eyes popped at the sight of a giant table loaded with a wide variety of luscious food, whiskey, and wine. Halina had baked a variety of cookies and cakes decorated with Christmas symbols. At the window, Christmas lights adorned a lamp. A tree decorated with gold and silver ornaments, including little bells and angels, sat in the middle of the living room. Bujalski and Halina sang Christmas carols.

We sat at the table and ate. We hadn't had such a meal in two years. Eddie stuffed himself with sweets. Never having eaten such food before and having listened to my mother's stories over and over, he asked, "Is the war over?"

Yitzchak smiled at his innocent question. "Not yet."

Bujalski wanted us to stay and talk with them. Halina was more friendly with us than she had been at any time before. After she had drunk a little, she stood next to me in the kitchen while I was filling my plate and leaned against me. No one else was in the kitchen. I knew she wanted me to kiss her. She was quite an attractive woman and I had not kissed a woman in a long time, but I knew that if Bujalski found out, he would be furious. He might order us from his farm, and then this wonderful night would turn to tragedy. The urge to live and to protect my family far outweighed my other urges. I just patted Halina on the shoulder and thanked her again for her generosity. But she was a beautiful woman and I was tempted.

We sat and talked until three o'clock in the morning, before we made our way cautiously back to the barn. Then the family discussed this strange night. Why had Bujalski been so generous to us on Christmas? Why all the food, and why in his house? The Christmas spirit? Was it because we seemed more human to him now that we explained that the difference between Jews and Christians was not so great? Because he

soon expected the war to end? Who knows. One takes kindness for what
it is sometimes and leaves it at that.

We dared to believe that we might survive. It was a strange but satisfying feeling for us.

On New Year's Day, 1944, the Bujalskis went to church and returned
with an extra ration of food for us. When he came to the barn, he stopped
to talk.

"People are still saying the war will soon end. I read an article in the
underground Polish newspaper urging Poles to help the Germans destroy any remaining Jews. The paper said that no witnesses should remain to testify about what has been done during the war years. I tell
you this because I wanted you to know that I don't hate Jews. After all,
aren't I hiding and feeding you?"

"Yes, you are and I want to thank you for your honesty and kindness."

Although this should not have come as any surprise to us, we still sat
and wondered how the same people with whom we had lived, worked,
and played could undertake to murder their fellow citizens, imitating
their bitter enemies who had instigated this extermination. It was incredible that they would cooperate with their conquerors in this geno-
cide. But such were the facts.

The days of winter slowly passed, filled with fear and hunger. It was
now quite cold outside, and even though we burrowed in the straw we
were chilled all the time. Our clothes had become worn and tattered
from continual wear, dirt, and sweat. We had nothing into which we
could change and nothing with which to patch the unwashed material.
We asked Bujalski for sewing needles. Then we opened the hems of our
shirts and trousers and removed some thread from the edges. The
women did the same with their clothes, using the thread to sew and darn
the holes.

The howling wind and blowing snow outside the barn ushered in the
month of February 1944. The February payment to Bujalski had nearly
exhausted our supply of gold coins. He, of course, did not know this,
but despite his kindnesses in recent weeks, it seemed unlikely that he
would continue to hide and feed us without generous compensation. We
would freeze to death in the forest or starve. The war could drag on
for another year or two.

So far we had survived by fleeing from hole to hole and attic to attic,
but then we still had money as a bargaining chip. Now, we were weaker,
had no money, and faced the bitter cold of February. Poles in the villages
awaited Jews coming to beg for food. They could be shot easily.

I looked at mother. What had become of her? She had been a respected
businesswoman who had owned a lumberyard, a clothing store, and two
brick buildings in the best location in the marketplace. She had owned
two apartment buildings. Now her only worldly possessions consisted of

an old tattered dress, a blouse, and an old pair of shoes. She was haggard and wrinkled and appeared to have aged twenty years. My nephew looked like a one-year-old, though he was well over three. He was emaciated and had no flesh on his bones.

How would we be able to survive in the cold forest without food and water? I lay awake all night, but I could think of nothing we could do to save ourselves. Even if I somehow survived the war, I did not think I would be strong enough to work and carry on a productive life. Rachel was gone. All my neighbors, relatives, friends, and acquaintances had been murdered—anyone who mattered was gone. The sight of my family's suffering multiplied the pain and grief. Something snapped. I had been stretched beyond my limits and I just could not go on. Rachel's death had left me nothing to live for; I was just delaying the inevitable. I saw no way out, except suicide. I decided to go down, run far enough into the forest so no one would know from where I had come, reveal myself to our Polish tormentors, and get myself shot.

In the morning we each got our share of bread and water. I could not eat. Yitzchak looked at me.

"Why aren't you eating?"

"I'm not hungry." Yitzchak and Paula were lying on the two boards that served as our door, and I said, "Will you move?"

"Why?"

"I'm going down."

"For what reason?"

"I have lived like this long enough. It is time to end it all." I pushed them aside and removed the boards, but they grabbed me and started to yell for the others. They held my legs, my mother held my shirt, and I was too weak to pull away. They replaced the boards.

"Feivel. The war will be over soon and we will be free. We have reasoned our way out of worse dilemmas, and we will be able to do so now. You don't want all of us to die just before being liberated."

I fell to the floor face down and cried. My mind was no longer functioning. I could not see a way out of our dilemma. I saw my mother crying. "Mother, I am sorry to trouble you so," I mumbled. I lay until it became dark. Everyone ate the piece of bread they had saved, but I had no appetite. I overheard mother talking quietly with my brother about watching me during the night, and she moved closer to the boards. She stayed up all night watching me.

I wracked my brain for a solution. Suddenly it occurred to me that we could offer Bujalski the apartment buildings, which had six tenants. Would he not rather live comfortably in town instead of working so hard on the farm? We could draw up a contract and have it notarized as soon as the war ended. I discussed this plan with the others, and they agreed it was an excellent idea. We did not want to give him our last bit of money.

When Bujalski arrived with some watery soup and bread, I asked, "Will you come up so we can talk?"

"All right." He came through the trap door and sat next to me.

"We no longer have gold with us, but we have more hidden in town. Because we can't go to Wegrow, we will draw up a contract stating that we are selling the houses to you in exchange for lodging and food."

He sat and thought. "I don't think such a contract will be considered legal after the war."

"Yes, it will. Pre-war laws will still apply after the war." He seemed unconvinced. "Take a day off and go to Warsaw with Halina, consult a lawyer there, and tell him that you have bought a house from a Jew whose location at present you do not know. Ask him if the contract will be valid after the war. Go to Warsaw instead of Wegrow, because if our name is mentioned in Wegrow, the people there will realize we are still alive. That could be fatal for both us and you."

He agreed and they left for Warsaw. They returned late at night and brought us some bread and milk.

"You are right. The lawyer in Warsaw told me that the contract is valid now and will be valid after the war." Bujalski was satisfied and accepted our arrangement, and we were allowed to continue to stay in his barn.

As March arrived, we yearned for the end of the war. Eddie, now four, was always hungry and we noticed a growth on his back, as large as a golfball and as hard as a rock. It was not painful, and we didn't know what it was, but we couldn't take him to a doctor. Jews were not supposed to be alive, let alone receiving medical care. After the war, we learned that it was a benign tumor. A Russian doctor removed it, leaving a large indentation on Eddie's back for the rest of his life.

On receiving our daily ration of bread, each of us would either eat it all at once or save part of it for later. Once, Yitzchak hung his piece of bread up on a wire so that the mice could not get at it. In the middle of the night, when Eddie could not sleep, my mother asked him what the problem was. He said he was hungry and asked her to give him a piece of Yitzchak's bread, but not to tell anyone. She agreed, and he fell asleep.

In the morning Yitzchak noticed his bread was missing and wondered how the mice could have gotten to it. Eddie feared his grandmother would tell what he had done, but of course she didn't.

In early April, Bujalski brought news of more Russian victories. We heard the sounds of airplanes overhead. He was now bringing very little bread, and Halina cooked a thin potato soup. For fear of arousing suspicion, he infrequently went to Wegrow for bread, and his wife was not baking. He told us his wife needed some leather shoes with wooden soles, but he couldn't afford to buy her new ones.

Especially now, when we were no longer paying him rent, we thought it was important to keep him as happy as possible. I told him that if he would bring me some wooden soles and some leather, I would make her a pair of shoes. If she liked them, I would make shoes for the children as well.

A few days later he brought me the materials, and I finished the shoes in a few days. She wore them to church on Sunday. After church they brought food and came up to talk. He continued to report that the war would soon end. He then said that his wife liked the shoes. People in the village had asked her where she had gotten them, and she told them in Warsaw. I again offered to make shoes for the children, hoping we might in return get a little extra bread or potatoes. I finished the shoes for the children, but our rations did not improve.

May arrived on a fine day. It was sunny outside and warm. I looked outside through the fist-sized hole that we had made for ventilation. Again I saw the cat and kittens stretched out in the sun and was envious of them. They could lie there freely, not a care in the world. Despite all the good news, I couldn't imagine we could ever be free like that again.

The food got worse. Bujalski must have felt he owed us less, because we were not paying him in cash. They cooked us soup with potatoes and farfel. It was more water than potatoes. We were hungry all the time. Eddie grew thinner and paler. He no longer said anything about being hungry.

Again we decided to go to Korczak at night and try to buy bread. He seemed pleased to see us. We told him we were still living in the forest. He gave us good news about the war, then he sold us two loaves of bread, each weighing ten pounds. We paid him and everyone was thrilled when we returned. Eddie got the first piece. Our spirits soared. Nightly, planes flew over. The front lines drew closer. By June, we had strong hopes.

III

On June 8, 1944, Bujalski told us that he had read in the underground newspaper that the Americans and the English had launched an invasion at Normandy in France two days earlier. Was he certain? He said he was. After eating our potatoes we talked about the powerful American weapons that would defeat the Germans. It was difficult to sleep that night because of the noise from the bombers overhead.

The next morning all was eerily quiet. Everything outside seemed undisturbed and peaceful. The rye and potatoes were as they had been. The barnyard animals seemed the same. Nothing had changed on the surface, but Bujalski seemed particularly excited when he brought us food that night.

On Sunday he returned from church with news that the Americans and English had advanced in the west, and the Russians in the east. The Germans were suffering tremendous losses. We relished this news. We knew it was in Bujalski's interest to keep us alive so he would get our houses.

Yitzchak and I went outside at night to see for ourselves what was going on. We looked up into the warm sky and saw blinking lights in the distance. We assumed these were military signals. Was the war really going to end?

In early July, Bujalski came to us with soup and bread, but he looked anxious.

"I have heard that as the Germans retreat, they burn all the barns, animals, and villages behind them, leaving nothing standing. Clearly, the war will not last long, but no one knows who will remain alive. My family may not survive. Perhaps, the property in Wegrow will be destroyed. I might end up with nothing for all the trouble of hiding you."

It was ironic. Our host had assumed death was only a worry for the Jews. Now, he feared for himself and his family, and he wasn't so nonchalant. Contemplating death was now a pastime of everyone, and he was finding it very uncomfortable. Well, welcome to the war, Mr. Bujalski!

But we also had a new danger. If the Germans burned our barn, we would die in the flames. We now had to remain alert at night. We stood watch in pairs outside in the grass each night all night, ready to alert the family to flee at a moment's notice. The winking stars formed a new roof and we took in a little fresh air. At dawn, we returned to the barn.

Would we see the end of the war, or be killed in its final days? It was a strange mixture of emotions for us. On the one hand, we had yearned for years to see the fall of Germany, and literally enjoyed hearing about German blood flowing in retribution for all the spilled Jewish blood. On the other hand, we had to worry about what awaited us at war's end. No friends. No money. No occupation. Nothing but neighbors who would like to see us dead, so the world could not know what they had done. Each Sunday, we sat impatiently waiting for Bujalski's news. He would bring us potato and farfel soup and then reveal the latest war news. The Americans were bombing Germany itself incessantly. The Germans were losing their best generals. They were retreating rapidly, but leaving charred villages behind. The Russians advanced. The Americans advanced. The Germans retreated.

We worried that Bujalski would forget to feed us, as he became more preoccupied. Each night, two family members sneaked into the fields to look for edibles. We found radishes, carrots, cucumbers, and lettuce, but took only a little at a time to prevent discovery of the thefts.

By August, the front had moved near. We heard that civilians, caught in the crossfire, had been injured or killed by shrapnel from bursting artillery shells. Everyone suffered losses, not just Jews. At night, a parade of bombers flew toward the Russian front. Excited, we thought the Messiah must be coming, but we didn't know how to greet Him.

We wanted to live to see how the world would look nearly devoid of Jews. For all our suffering, we wanted to be there at the end. Bujalski said he was going to flee to a neighborhing village when the Russians came. If he heard that his village was not burned, he would return. But if it had been destroyed, he would continue fleeing.

In early September we heard voices near the house. I looked out and recognized Bujalski and Halina talking with his brother and sister-in-law. They had not spoken to each other since our arrival. Other neighbors were there, too. Bujalski later told us they had discussed whether to stay and be prepared to extinguish fires set by the Germans, or flee and wait for the results. They had not settled on a plan.

If they all fled, we could not join them. They would kill us. But if we stayed, we might burn to death.

The next day an agitated Bujalski stopped by. "Halina and I have decided to take the family to the in-laws in a village about thirty kilometers away. We are going to wait there and see what the Germans do. I can no longer help you. I wouldn't stay in the barn, because the dry straw roof will burn quickly. I'd go into the rye fields with the bundles. Spread out among the different bundles, and I will bring you bread and water until I leave. I am going to release the cows and pigs into the fields so they will not be burned in the barn." As he said goodbye, we saw tears fill his eyes. Were they tears for us or themselves?

Late that night, we crept outside, each with a piece of bread in his pocket, and carefully walked far out into the rye fields. We planned how we would be arranged. I would be with my mother, Yitzchak would be with one child and Paula with another, Yerachmiel with Itke, and Moshe with Menucha. We spread apart and remained quiet, so as not to be detected by the neighbors.

During the night we heard bursting artillery shells, but could not tell how far away. The next afternoon we heard footsteps nearing. I tensed ready to fight. It was Bujalski.

"Heard anything?"

"The front is very near. The Germans arrive first, closely followed by the Russians. I'm afraid of the Russians."

"They could be no worse than the Germans."

"The key to my house is hidden near the window sill. You can go there after dark to get some more bread."

After he left, we remained in the rye bundles, baking in the sun. In the evening, we left the bundles to cool off in the night air. All was quiet. At the house, we found the bread, sliced it, and took it back to the field along with some water. We ate and sat out until light.

Later in the week, Bujalski came again to check on his cows and pigs.

"How are you doing?"

"We are still alive."

"The Germans are fortifying and concentrating their artillery about a kilometer away. If they bombard the Russians from there, the Russians will respond and everything will likely be destroyed!"

"Where can we go?"

"There is nowhere to run to. Goodbye. I wish you well."

We discussed our situation and came to the conclusion that we could do nothing. We were now in God's hands. We stayed in the rye. At dawn, Yitzchak saw a flock of crows near the horizon.

"Do you see the same thing?"

"Yes, I do." As we watched the "crows" approaching, we saw that they were people! They approached from surrounding fields, like locusts, closer and closer. We could tell they were soldiers, but we couldn't tell whose. A few minutes later Yitzchak yelled, "They are Russian! Let's go and tell them we are here."

"Stay put. The soldiers have machine guns and grenades. They are advancing quickly with their heads low. If we should suddenly appear, they will likely shoot us before we can identify ourselves. Everyone, hold onto the bundles tightly so they do not fall down as the Russians pass by."

They came by the hundreds, swarming through the fields. A soldier pushed against our bundle, and had I not been holding it up firmly, it would have fallen. It was incredible. We were actually in the middle of a battlefield, and no one knew we were there. One side was fleeing while the other was taking over the territory left behind. This was the front! On and on, the soldiers came, so close we could have reached out and touched them. I felt, excitement, fear, exhilaration, and hope all at one time.

At night we lay still and the commotion subsided. The Germans are defeated! The Germans are beaten! The war in Poland is over! The Nazis are gone. It's over. Over. It's over. We can go home.

The day that we had long awaited had finally arrived, but to be certain, we remained in the rye field. Early in the morning, not having to fear the Germans' burning the barn, we returned to our hiding place. Although we had gotten no rest all night, we could not sleep. We were too excited. Our joy was unbounded. We were finally seeing what we had yearned and prayed to see—the defeat of Hitler. It would be a shame to sleep away such a moment.

In the morning Bujalski came back to find his property intact. This pleased him, but he was not happy with the coming of the Russians. The Poles feared the Russians. They thought the communists would take over their farms and enslave them. They were right. They had not suffered much under the Germans, but Bujalski and all his friends would lose their farms and homes to the Marxists, who would communize the entire country. He told us to remain in the hiding place until he could be certain that the Germans would not return.

That evening, he told us that the Russians had advanced to Praga, on the Vistula River near Warsaw. On the other side of the river were the Germans. We asked Bujalski to go to Wegrow and find out what the situation was there, whether it was safe for us to return home. Impatiently, we waited. He returned in a few hours. "Wegrow is full of Russian soldiers. The city has not been damaged by bombs or shells. Your buildings are still standing, but all the stores in town are closed."

"Bujalski. It is time for us to go home. You will be free of us and won't have to feed us any longer. Will you accompany us home in the morning?"

"Yes, but we will have to leave at four o'clock in the morning so that the neighbors do not see me transporting Jews."

"We will be ready."

Chapter 8

What Do You Say to Murderers?

I

It was mid-September 1944. At four o'clock we nervously left the barn to return to Wegrow. We were nervous because we were returning to a town which was, as the Nazis said, *Judenrein* (clean of Jews). We had no idea what such a town would offer us. Who would we talk to? All our close friends and relatives were dead. Should we open our store for business as usual and chat with the customers as they came in?

Hello. How are you? Lovely day. How are your wife and the little ones? Has your back been hurting you lately? I heard your fine bull died last week. Sorry to hear that. You will find another. Do you think the crops will be good this year? Seems like we had plenty of rain. What can I get for you today? Some shirts? Trousers? We have a beautiful selection, just delivered today. I believe you are a 38 short, aren't you?

Could such a conversation with these people ever be possible? Could I open the shop and return to business, as usual, forgetting everything from the past?

What do you say to murderers?

How would the people of Wegrow react to seeing my family back in town? Would they come up to me and tell me how sorry they were, and how tragic it all was? Would they ignore us? Would they try to kill us to keep us from telling the world what really happened? I didn't know, but one thing was certain—I would never forget. They could count on that. Never! From the people of Wegrow, I had come to expect nothing but the worst, and there was nothing anyone could do to me or my family that would surprise me. What I had left was what I knew and what I would tell.

We all got into Bujalski's wagon and set out along the main road, traveling slowly at first and then picking up speed as we left the village so we would arrive before dawn. We looked about studiously, noting that the world somehow appeared different than before. It had been five long years—maybe the longest five years anyone on earth ever spent—but it was over. I swore that my family would never live in hiding ever again.

Near town, we climbed from the wagon to walk the rest of the way. Bujalski continued into town, so no one would know he had traveled with Jews. Mother, however, could not walk, and she rode into town with him, dressed to look like a peasant woman in a dress and shawl Bujalski had loaned her.

Russian soldiers, trucks, and tanks filled the city's streets. Mother left the wagon at the front of our yard, and we arrived a few minutes later. There was the house and store in front of us with the door closed, just as it had stood for seven centuries.

I opened the door and entered. A foul smell met me. It was a mixture of the odors of vodka, wine, champagne, cigar smoke, and perfume. The Polish women had caroused in our house with German soldiers, certain that the building's former occupants had met their doom in the ovens. Suddenly, the thought of entering my own house sickened me. It had been defiled.

I stood before the door a moment and then went inside. The place had been completely stripped. No tables, no chairs, no glasses, no utensils, no beds, no wall decorations. Nothing. Only four empty walls. Mother could not stand on her feet long, and she lay down on the floor. She had nothing on which she could even rest her head.

We said goodbye to Bujalski and thanked him for everything. Because the war was not yet over, and because parts of Poland were still occupied by the Germans, he could not yet legally take possession of our apartment buildings. Nevertheless he was glad that our house still stood, and that no one had discovered that he had hidden Jews. He left contented.

I ventured into the yard and looked around the outside of the house and store. A section of the roof had been torn away by shrapnel, but that seemed to be a minor problem at the moment. We had no money, no food, and no cooking utensils—nothing even to carry water.

Russian military vehicles had camped in the backyard between the house and the lumberyard, and a Russian field kitchen provided food for the soldiers.

I spied some Red Army soldiers in the field kitchen and walked over to the cook.

"My family and I have just returned home. Can you give us a little food?"

"Do you live in this house?"

"I lived here with my family."

"Why do you look so thin and frail?"

"We are Jews, who have been in hiding throughout the war in the fields and forests. The Germans sought to kill us, and we have been unable to find adequate nourishment in hiding."

"Do you have any food?"

"No food and no money."

"Get a pot and I will give you some of the food I am cooking here."

"We have no pots or utensils of any kind."

Astonished, he said, "You have nothing?"

"Nothing."

"Wait. I'll give it to you in one of my pots."

He scrounged through his truck and took out a pot, some plates, rusty spoons, and a hunk of black bread. Filling the pan with food, he handed it to me, along with a pitcher of water. I thanked him profusely and carried it all back to the house.

Everyone was overjoyed. We ate our first meal in freedom. Then I returned the utensils to the cook, and Moshe and I stood in front of the store, watching the Russian soldiers parade through the streets. Few civilians appeared. From a distance, in the square, some Poles stared at us in disbelief, but no one approached.

Standing there, I began to hear a buzzing in my ears, as if bees were flying around my head. This sound remained with me for about a month. It must have been the lack of nourishment and my frail condition. When we tired of standing, we returned to the house to join the family and sat on the floor until nightfall. Then we all fell into fitful sleep, tossing from side to side on the hard floor. At dawn, we awoke. I did not know what our first day of freedom would be like, but, as it turned out, it wasn't much.

As I strolled outside, the Russian cook immediately spotted me and called me over. "I have breakfast for you." He gave me a tureen of soup, two plates, and two spoons. I thanked him very much, and as we ate, we thanked God that the Russian kitchen had parked in our yard.

After breakfast, Moshe and I crossed the street to the marketplace. Again, we saw Poles standing off at a distance, staring in disbelief. They knew us well, but they did not have the decency to come over and ask how we were or if we needed anything. I saw Pierkowski, the one who had hidden Menucha in his small barn after she had been shot, and who had stored some of our valuables. He stood there, tall and strong. I was so excited to see him that I ran over to him, grabbed his hand and bent down to kiss it. Suddenly he shoved me away firmly, rejecting me. I looked up to see what had happened. I saw the Poles standing and looking at us. I understood. Pierkowski had to push me away because he was ashamed to let them see a Jew getting so close to him. I left with my head bowed and walked back home. We never got back the personal belongings we had left with him.

I told the others what had happened. The incident affected me profoundly. My chest felt tight, and my eyes began to tear. Even the people who had helped us were afraid to show us kindness in public. Was it possible that in the entire world we had not a single friend? Could a man continue to exist this way? I went over to a corner of the house and asked God, "Master of the universe, why did You create me?" There was no answer, but I felt better just saying aloud what was on my mind.

At noon I went out again, and the Russian cook told me he had lunch ready. Daily, the cook gave us food. At least one person in the world had pity on us.

Freedom did not bring happiness. We were sad and depressed and longed to see another Jew. It just seemed wrong. I imagined that if I went to the marketplace, I would find some neighbor of ours with whom I could chat. Someone besides us had to be left from the Jewish community. I stood in front of the store for hours at a time hoping to see a familiar Jewish face. On the right Simcha Kukawka, Shlomo Laufer, Velvel Lass, Yechezekiel Zilberman, Simcha Lazewnik, Yechezkiel Schlezinger, Laizer Finkelstein, Alter Bergman, Laizer Laufman, and Boruch Morgenstern had all lived. On the left had been Fishel Chudzik, Hersch Laizer Chudzik, Shmuel Moncarz, Moshe Steinberg, Pesach Rosenbaum, Hershel Recant, Rosa and Wolf Tick, Yitzchak Shochet Szydlowski, Yosef Shochet, Yaakov Baumgarten, Sholom Radziminski, Yosef Chaim Borenstein, the Zlotowski family with their children Sarah and Rachel, Hershel Felsher Weintraub, Nathan Weintraub, the Kawers, Nisman the dentist, Laizer Reszes, Eliyahu Grenstein, and the Zajonc family. I waited for them to appear. I waited the entire day, but I saw not a single one of them. I saw only the Poles walking on the street. They looked at us bitterly from a distance. No one approached us.

Stubbornly my brother and I stood outside the entire day. When our legs grew weary from standing, we sat down on the pavement until it became dark. We re-entered the house, my ears still buzzing. We sat on the floor like mourners sitting *shiva* just after a person has died. We were sitting *shiva* for the millions of our brothers and sisters.

It struck me: We could sit on that front porch all month and nothing would change. We would see no other Jews. We were the last Jews from Wegrow. Although I didn't know it then, I was not completely right. Other Jews would return, but only to leave again. In another year, all the Jews would truly be gone.

After a fitful night's sleep, I returned to the mess tent, where the Russian again greeted me with food.

"Here, take it," he said jovially. "If you don't take it, someone else will."

For days, we stayed alone, shunned. Only Bujalski came from time to time to see how we were—and probably to keep an eye on his property. All stores and restaurants remained closed. The Russian soldiers asked me where they could find a restaurant or bar to get a drink of vodka, but no place was open. The Poles feared the Russians.

I waited to see if any Jews would arrive to go to the synagogue for afternoon and evening services and listen to an itinerant rabbi. No one appeared. We saw only the Poles, who so recently had wanted to kill us and rob us. They passed us and looked impudently at us. I almost envied the dead. They no longer had to look at the faces of these murderers. I thought long and hard about our future. Were we to exist in a world full of such hate for us?

I came to the conclusion that life was not worth living. I again contemplated suicide, but told no one in the family. I had learned that it was a sin to commit suicide, but I could not get the images of these murderers out of my mind, these people who had shot Jews for two pounds of sugar and their clothes. I could not stand to see them walking the street unpunished.

The next day something happened to change my mind. A handful of Jews returned to Wegrow—Shmuel Rajzman, a woman friend, and Shmuel Wilenberg. They had hidden with a Christian family. Shmuel Rajzman had been a bookkeeper in the Warsaw ghetto and had survived working in the concentration camp. He escaped on August 2, 1943, during the Treblinka uprising, along with Wilenberg, a Jew from Czenstechow. Rajzman, who had helped organize the uprising, told me about how trains entered Treblinka packed with Jews, how he had watched his mother forced to undress, and how he had stacked her clothes in piles with the rest before she was shot. He had seen the great Aleksander Rebbe, Yitzchak Menachem, forced to undress. Noticing some small children nearby, the Rebbe took one in his arm and challenged God, "Master of the universe, I have sinned, but what have these innocent children done?" The SS shot him on the spot and dumped his naked body into a mass grave with countless other bodies of men and women. Rajzman later testified in 1947 in the Nuremberg Nazi war criminal trials.

Each day, another Jew or two returned. A young couple, Irving and Chaya Wenger, had been kept by a gentile and worked as carpenters. They later emigrated to the United States, and we remain friends today. Yitzchak Kreda, the launderer's son, had been hidden by a Polish girl.

They trickled back, bedraggled, bloody, starved, and destitute. They had hidden in the forests and fields, or had fought with the partisans. A total of about sixty or seventy returned, all that was left of 6,000.

Most stopped by to see us. Our house became the meeting place, and we fed them as best we could from the Russian Army kitchen. The Jews returned to Wegrow, but none knew why, except that they still had nowhere else to go. Yet, now that there were people I could talk to, I abandoned by thoughts of suicide.

II

Four weeks had passed since the Soviet soldiers had driven the Nazis from Wegrow. We realized it was fruitless to sit and do nothing, existing on the generosity of the Russian cook. If the mobile kitchen moved, or the Russians left, we would be left with nothing. I thought that if we opened a restaurant and tavern, we could earn a living feeding the Red Army soldiers. We would need bread, vegetables, some meat, and, most importantly, vodka. With no money, this presented a challenge.

I asked the mayor if the city would repair our damaged roof, because we had no money. He agreed. I asked Bujalski if he would provide vodka on credit and I would repay him with interest. He agreed. The next day he brought me a gallon. I obtained bread from a baker, to-matoes from a grocer, dinnerware from a gentile neighbor, and an old table and chairs from another neighbor, promising to pay for the food later.

My restaurant opened for business. Within five minutes a group of Russian soldiers entered and asked for vodka. One asked for a hundred grams. I didn't know how much that was, so he told me to fill a glass. He asked how much it cost. I said one ruble, and he paid without hes-itation. He gulped it down and ordered another, along with a piece of bread and a tomato. Two rubles. He paid. Before long, I had a flour-ishing business. Soldiers came in demanding, "Give me vodka!"

Seeing how freely they were throwing their money around, I knew that my prices were too low, so I tripled them, but still I could not pour fast enough. Within two hours, I was sold out. Soldiers filled the house, milling about and demanding vodka. I promised them that I would have more the next day, and they all grudgingly left.

I closed up and contacted Bujalski, who promised two and a half gallons for me the next day. The baker refused to accept the Russian money, thinking it would be worthless. I explained that as long as the Russians remained here, their money would be legal tender. He nodded and took the rubles. I bought four loaves, then went to the grocer and purchased eleven pounds of tomatoes. I also learned that a glass was considerably more than a hundred grams.

I opened the next day, and the soldiers rushed in ordering a hundred grams, two hundred grams, one after the other. I charged four rubles a glass, upping my prices another 33 percent. They paid willingly, and again I was sold out. I kept restocking, reassuring my suppliers that Russian money would be the real money. In this way we earned enough to support ourselves.

A few weeks passed, and I began to feel better about living. We had managed to save some money. The few Jews who returned told us what they had lived through. None had hidden in as many places as we had.

During this time, a man named Morris Abarbanel came wandering into the restaurant. He was a religious Jew who had hidden in the forests with his brother during the war and had survived. He looked quite haggard and emaciated. His family had all perished, including his brother who could not survive against the elements. Morris had heard that a family of Jews operated a restaurant in Wegrow and came to see if he could find kosher food. He had had some relatives in Wegrow before the war. He refused to eat anything but kosher meat, and none could be had in most areas of Poland, because not enough Jews were left in most places to keep a kosher butcher busy.

We found food for him and a place to stay. He and Menucha became close, and only three weeks later, in November 1944, they married. I felt happy for Menucha, who had experienced nothing but misery since she was twenty. Now at age twenty five, she had found someone with whom she could spend her life. They had a Jewish wedding, the last one in Wegrow, and Morris stayed with us.

We heard that a Jewish Committee had formed in Praga near Warsaw. Word came that all Jews who had survived should register, organize, vote for local committees, and elect officers. The Jews in Wegrow met in our house and elected me president. I traveled to Praga for the meeting of the central committee, where I received a seal of office. The committee told me to report any problems or questions from the Jews in Wegrow.

While in Praga, I found a store that sold Russian food. A friend from Warsaw worked there as a salesman, and the store gladly accepted Russian money. I bought sardines, cheese, cigarettes, flatware, and glasses. I came home loaded with the supplies. I then bought used furniture, returning the borrowed supplies to the neighbors.

In no time, word got around that there was a real restaurant in town. I sold sardines, cheese, bread, tomatoes, eggs, and vodka. No one else in town sold cigarettes. Little by little, the Poles also began to come in. Those who had tried to kill us came in and told us how sorry they were that the Germans had killed the Jews. They told us what fine people the Jews were.

Even Saszym, the one who had hidden mother for a time and who had later tried to kill me, came in about six months after I had come back to town, in early 1945.

"Welcome, welcome, Saszym. Sit down at a table here." I put food and vodka on the table. "Everything is on the house. This is a reward for keeping my mother and because you are such a fine man." He ate, drank, and then talked.

Finally he asked, "Are you angry with me?"

"You are my best friend. If all people were as good as you, the world would be a better place."

I hid my true feelings, because he could have easily killed me. Many Poles killed Jews, even after the Russians' arrival. They were afraid that the Jews would testify against them and tell the Russians that they had cooperated with the Germans in the slaughter of the Jews. I wanted Saszym as a "friend."

About a week later, we found Yitzchak Kreda's body in the woods. He had survived the war, been liberated, and seen the Russians arrive. Yet, he had no work and no place to go. His father's laundry had been taken over by a Pole, whom his father had trained. Yitzchak had gone to the Pole's house and asked him to return part of the business to him. The Pole took out a revolver and shot him. He dragged the body into the woods and left it there. We found it and gave him a Jewish burial.

Another young Jew, Feivel Szpilman, survived the war and returned to Wegrow before settling in Seidlce. A week later, we heard that a Pole had shot him. We heard of many such examples in which Jews had survived the hell of the war, only to be killed by their Polish countrymen after they had returned home. As the Jews of the smaller villages heard these reports, they began to migrate to the larger towns, such as Lodz. They were more secure in larger groups.

In the spring of 1945, a young man wearing a university cap came into the restaurant, accompanied by two pretty blonde girls. "Can you help us? We heard that a Jew in Wegrow survived the war and opened a restaurant. We have not seen Jews for a long time and we want to see what one looks like."

"My name is Shraga Feivel Bielawski. I own this restaurant and I am Jewish."

We talked for a while and they left. About an hour later, one of the girls came running back, upset and nervous. She had noticed the back door to the building and asked me to go back there with her. She said she had something important to tell me.

Inside, she said, "My name was Lusia Lieberman. I am from Bialystok, where my parents had a business selling gold, silver, and watches. The Germans killed my entire family, but I escaped. Because I do not look Jewish, I went to Warsaw dressed as a Pole, with a forged Polish passport identifying me as a Christian. I worked in a Polish restaurant where students came in often to eat. I met a young student there and we became engaged. I really honestly thought that there were no Jews left in all of Europe. When I heard that a Jewish family had survived and was operating a restaurant in Wegrow, I remembered who and what I was. I asked my fiancé to take me to see what a Jew looked like. He became intrigued, and he and his sister accompanied me to Wegrow. After seeing you, I realized that I did not want to live as a gentile. I want to live with my people."

At the truck station, waiting for the return to Warsaw, she had noticed an outside restroom. She then excused herself, went into the restroom, and sneaked away to our store. Now, she pleaded with me to save her.

I never would have guessed that she was Jewish, but I told her to stay in the house behind locked doors and I would try to think of something. I had been unable to explain why I was still alive. So many lucky breaks and close calls and still I lived to see the Nazis driven from Wegrow. Why? The question had not left my mind. Of course, I had used my wits to stay alive, but certainly there were people much smarter than I who had not survived. Why me? God had allowed me to live for some reason. Was this why? To keep the flame of 4,000 years burning? To see that there would be a tomorrow for the Jews? I could easily have declined to help. The fiancé would be angry. He might even think the woman had left him for me. But perhaps this was now my sole reason for existence, and I felt I had to do it. I thought back to the passage from my Hebrew studies, "If someone saves one life, it is as if he had saved an entire world!" I was now determined to save her with all the means at my disposal.

She stayed in the house and left for Praga by truck at four o'clock in the morning. I gave her enough money to buy the ticket and to cover a few days' expenses, and I wrote a letter of explanation to the Jewish Committee, asking them to care for her.

I heard nothing from her until about a month later, when I took mother to Praga to stay with some friends. When I stepped into the offices of the Jewish Committee to check on the young lady, a girl suddenly ran up to me, embraced me, and kissed me. This was the same girl! The committee had given her a job as a secretary. She had met a Jewish engineer, they had married, and she was very happy. She thanked me repeatedly.

III

Weeks passed and the restaurant prospered. With our profits I purchased proper dinnerware and kitchenware. We bought clothing and bedding, and our food was sufficient for our needs.

But we still felt uncomfortable and unsafe in Wegrow. By the time the war officially ended in Europe in May 1945, the Jews of Wegrow had begun to leave for Warsaw, Lodz, and Bytom. Yitzchak and his family moved to Bytom, Yerachmiel and Itke to Lodz, and mother later moved to Praga. Only Moshe, Menucha, and I remained to run the restaurant.

We realized that we, too, would have to leave eventually, but for the time being, we were earning a living. Occasionally, Poles would come into the restaurant and get drunk. One of them called me over one day.

"Do you know where the big synagogue is?"

"The synagogue no longer exists, but I don't know what happened to it."

"The priest bought the synagogue from the Germans and we tore the building apart. We used the bricks to build a wall around the Catholic cemetery. What do you think of that, Jew boy?"

My stomach wrenched. This is what had become of our beautiful synagogue, the place where I had sat in awe as a boy. The other smaller synagogues still stood, but we had barely enough men for a minyan. The Great Synagogue was now a wall for a Catholic cemetery.

At the end of June, six women came into the restaurant, sunburned, barefoot, and dirty. They looked around.

"May I help you?"

"Are you a Jew?"

"Yes."

They began to speak in Yiddish. "We would like to speak with you privately." I led them into the house and closed the door behind us.

Four of the women were single and the other two were mother and daughter. The mother told me their story: "We come from Russia by way of Liv (a few miles from Wegrow). When the Germans drove into the Soviet Union in 1941, we were sent to Germany to work in a factory. After the Red Army invaded Germany, all Soviet citizens were ordered back to Russia for labor. The Red Army also took from occupied Germany as much material, food, and machinery as their trucks could carry, but there were not enough trucks. They told the people to lead the cattle back to the Soviet Union on foot, and we have been driving the cattle all the way from Germany. Two soldiers have been assigned to guard us and prevent our escape. For four weeks we have been driving the cattle in the rain and the heat. At night we sleep in the open."

As she told me the story, they all began to cry. "We do not want to return to Russia. Please help us."

I again wondered if God were testing me to see if I would be willing to put myself in jeopardy to save others. Again I thought of the passage in my studies. "Can you spend the night here?"

"We have to return now, but we will sneak away in the middle of the night."

"I have a plan, but you will have to keep it secret. No one else must know. I will buy you six tickets for the truck to Praga and write a letter to the Jewish Committee there. You will have to be here before the truck leaves at 6:00 a.m." They agreed and left.

I stayed awake all night worrying. If the Russians found out about this, they would shoot all of them and me as well. At 5:45 a.m. they appeared at the house, and I led them out the back door. Fortunately, the truck station was nearby. I gave them the tickets and the letter and told them to take seats away from the windows of the truck, because they would be traveling through the same area where the herds of cattle were. I wished them luck and they left.

Around noon that day, two Russian soldiers opened the door to my restaurant, looked inside, and left. I watched as they checked all the stores on the street. In the afternoon I saw the same two soldiers leading a herd of cattle through town. I realized that these were the soldiers who had guarded the women. Now they had to lead the cattle themselves.

The following week I went to Praga to see the committee. As soon as I went inside, I saw one of the women leave and return with the other five. They grabbed me and lifted me up in the air, shouting, "Long live Mr. Bielawski!" They held me aloft for a few minutes. The other people there didn't know what was going on until the women explained.

I asked how they were. One had found her father, and another had found a brother. They were all happy that they had been saved from the hands of the Russians. They told me they had all decided to make their way to Palestine to live. They warmly thanked me and said goodbye as I left. I felt as if the five years of hiding were worth something. It wasn't really much, but this small gesture made me feel like a human being again.

While I was there, I traveled to Warsaw to get more goods for the restaurant. I had not been in Warsaw in three years, and while the rubble still lay in heaps, I knew the city had changed. No Jews. I did not stay there long. Too many memories to forget.

My business continued to increase, and soon members of the security police started to patronize the restaurant. These were Poles whom the Russians had enlisted. Any Pole who professed to be a communist could apply to serve in the *Ubezpieczenstwa*, the security police force at the city hall. Most were the same cutthroats who had helped the Germans kill

Jews. Now they were security police. This prompted even more Jews to leave Wegrow.

One day around noon one of the security police came into the restaurant as Moshe played his accordion to entertain the customers. He came over to Moshe and demanded the accordion.

I intervened. "That belongs to my brother." He scowled at me, looked me up and down, and then slapped me across the face. My face became red and swollen. Then he turned and left.

The restaurant grew quiet. The patrons advised me to go to the commanding officer and tell him what had happened. The man had assaulted me for no reason. They even offered to testify on my behalf.

I went to the station and encountered about twenty police.

"I'd like to see the chief. One of your colleagues attacked me."

"The chief is not here. You will have to wait."

I waited about twenty minutes. The man who had hit me then came in and saw me. "What is he doing here?"

"He is going to report you to the chief." Hearing this he lunged at me, beating me until I fell to the floor. I lay there thinking that I would not leave the place alive, but he left.

About half an hour later I heard the telephone ring. Someone answered, and then one of the officers came over, picked me up, and told me to leave. I rose and started for the door, looking back to see if they were going to shoot me.

At home, Moshe said that when I had not returned promptly, he called the mayor and told him about the incident in the restaurant. He asked the mayor to find out what had happened to me and get me released.

The time had again come for us to leave everything behind and run. I feared that the security policeman would return to take his revenge. The next day, through the window, I saw a policeman carrying a machine gun. He staggered, obviously drunk, as he walked toward the house, so I immediately locked the door. He knocked on the door, looked in the window, and finally left.

I told Moshe, Menucha, and Morris we had to move quickly. We decided we would each pack suitcases with necessities and leave town on the truck for Warsaw at four o'clock the next morning. We would leave everything else behind once again, after so much hard work. I had started this business a year earlier without a cent and had built it into a successful restaurant, equipped with good furniture, dishes, food, and drink. Now we had to leave it all and flee. How many times would this recur? We toiled and built, only to leave it all to save our lives.

The next morning, we boarded the truck and left Wegrow. No Jews remained. As I stepped up to the bed of the truck, I carried 700 years of history with me. I never looked back. I kept my eyes forward and concentrated on the road in front of me. The town had won. The Poles and Germans had not killed all the Jews. Some had lived, but they all had left.

Bujalski had gotten all our property, except for the house and store, and I never learned what happened to our home. I never visited Korczak after we left Bujalski's barn. I wanted to, but he lived so far away and I never had the chance. He never came to town. I think of him often, and I wish him well.

But something happened that day. That morning in October 1945, just after World War II had ended, four Jews carrying suitcases climbed aboard a truck. No one noticed, but this was as significant as any event in the history of the town. Centuries of tradition died. As the gears shifted and the tires turned, kicking up dust in the pre-dawn air, the houses of the city around me faded and were replaced by the fields and forests. The place where I had lived all my life, and where my mother's family had lived for generations, became only a memory. My sister, her husband, my brother, and I left for good. We never returned. I was the last Jew from Wegrow.

IV

We stayed only briefly in Warsaw and soon departed for Lodz to join Yerachmiel and Itke. My mother had suffered heart problems and had remained bedridden since leaving the hiding place. She moved to Lodz to be with my brother, but the city had few good doctors or pharmacies after the war, and she stayed in bed for an entire year, showing no improvement.

We did not believe Poland offered anything for Jews. With all that we had suffered, more attacks came. Scattered pogroms broke out in Poland, placing the few Jews left there under attack. Amazingly, some Poles blamed the Jews for the war.

By now, Yitzchak and Paula had left Bytom to go to Germany to find the refugee camps for Jews sponsored by the United Nations and the United States. Many hoped to emigrate to the United States or to Palestine. Yerachmiel and Itke decided to go to Berlin to a refugee camp funded by UNRWA—the United Nations Relief and Works Agency. Menucha and Morris followed them to Berlin. Moshe, mother, and I remained behind in Lodz, until late in 1945 when Moshe met a boyhood friend, Yerachmiel Zulte. Zulte had left Wegrow before the war to go to Palestine, where he enlisted in the Jewish Brigade of the British Army and had fought against the Germans. After the war he returned to Wegrow to search for any surviving family members. Dressed in military fatigues, he brought an extra uniform. He thought he might find at least one surviving relative and smuggle him out in the extra uniform, but no one from his family was left. By chance, he met Moshe in Lodz and offered him the chance to go to Belgium dressed as a soldier. His brigade was temporarily stationed there.

Moshe accepted. There he met a cousin, Leah Shlessinger, who had lived in Brussels in hiding throughout the war. Together, they obtained a temporary visa for me and mother to come to Belgium. But we could not leave.

Mother's health failed day by day. The thought of leaving Poland pleased her, because she knew she didn't have long to live. She had told me that she did not want to be buried in Poland, in ground which had been soaked with so much innocent Jewish blood, but she became too weak to make the journey. I had to remain with her in Lodz.

During this time, a cousin of my sister-in-law Paula came to where we were living in Lodz to pay her respects. Her name was Esther Gold. Paula's mother and Esther's father were brother and sister. Esther had hidden throughout the war in a small town, Pinczow, near Cracow. She and her family had survived, and when she heard we were living in Lodz, she stopped by. Esther and I had known each other before the war, but we had never dated, because Rachel had always been my single interest. Now, it was good to have someone like Esther around, who knew Rachel and understood how I felt, but who also could provide warmth and companionship. We grew closer and dated for two months. She was not Rachel. No one would ever be Rachel, but Esther was a wonderful, kind, attractive person, and I desperately needed her. She needed me, too.

In January 1946, my mother died. Moshe returned from Belgium for the funeral, and we buried her in Lodz with a simple tombstone by her grave. It is generally accepted by historians that 6 million Jews died at the hands of the Nazis, but, of course, many more uncounted Jews died of starvation or exposure, and still other thousands, like my mother, just were never the same again. In most cases, only the young and strong, who managed to elude their persecutors, lived for more than a few years, and they carried with them horrible mental scars.

I remained in Poland only eight days longer. We sat *shiva*, mourning my mother's death for seven days, but I could not wait to leave. On the one hand, it felt strange to leave the land of my birth, the place where I had grown up with my childhood friends and family. My family had been in Poland for over 300 years. I would not have imagined that I would leave all my roots behind and go to a strange country.

On the other hand, how could I remain in a place where I had witnessed Jews led to their deaths by their neighbors? This place did not want me, and I could no longer stomach it. I was bitter. I prayed that the land would split and swallow up the Poles as Korach's followers were swallowed by the earth in the days of Moses. Poland held nothing but foul memories.

I packed my belongings into two suitcases. Moshe and I took a bus to Warsaw and then a train to Brussels. Just as when I left Wegrow, I kept my eyes forward and never looked back. The fields and cities of Poland whizzed by the train window in a blur. The Polish border crossing took only a few hours, and I never returned to my homeland again.

In Brussels, lodging was scarce, but Moshe had made friends with people who helped us find an apartment within a few days.

I then searched for a job. I had business sense, but no marketable trade or craft, and I had to compete with a stream of other refugees. I realized that I would have to learn a trade, and so I decided to pursue a job in a ladies' handbag factory. I worked long hours in a hot attic for minimal pay, but I learned how to make handbags and how to fashion new styles.

Esther had emigrated with her family to Munich in occupied Germany, because it was much less difficult for Jews to emigrate from Germany to the United States than from other parts of Europe. Belatedly, the United States had opened its arms to the Jews, who had suffered under Nazi persecution, and with the United States Army occupying part of Germany, this emigration process was most easily accomplished from there. I decided to go to Munich to see her, and to explore the possibility of emigrating. With a two-week visa, I boarded a train and arrived a few hours later. Esther was living with her brother David and mother Hannah in a one-room apartment. Her older sister, Shoshana, had boarded a ship that carried Jews illegally to Palestine. Esther worked as a secretary in the UNRWA office, which distributed food and money to war refugees.

I learned that the Jews presently in the refugee camps in Germany had first priority to emigrate to other Allied countries. If I were to apply for emigration to the United States now, I would have to wait a few more years. At the end of my two-week stay, I returned to Belgium where living conditions were better. I enjoyed Belgium. It was free, clean, and relatively prosperous. The people were friendly and polite. I remained in Belgium, but I kept up a correspondence with Esther.

After working in the handbag factory for eighteen months and mastering the art of designing and making handbags, I decided to open my own factory. But the local authorities said only native Belgians could obtain permits to open factories. I had pinned my hopes on being able to better myself, and I was disappointed.

In early 1949, after living in Belgium for two years, Moshe and I decided to return to Germany to apply for emigration to the United States. Esther arranged for an elderly German couple to house me and provide me with a legitimate address in Munich-Pasing at Fritz Reuter Strasse #2.

Esther and I dated more seriously for a few months, and we decided to get married. It was difficult to let go of Rachel's memory, but she would not have wanted me to be alone and miserable all my life. Esther knew how I felt, and she understood. We would marry, but Rachel's memory would never die. Never. They had killed her, but she would live on as long as I had a memory.

We discussed the time and place of the wedding. We could marry in Munich, in Frankfurt where Menucha was living, or in Bergen-Belsen, the location of the infamous German death camp. Esther's cousin, Eva Radziejewski, lived there with her husband Roman.

After careful thought, we decided on Bergen-Belsen. We would be wed near where countless thousands of Jewish men, women, and children had been slaughtered by the Nazis. We had clung stubbornly to life. Now, we would marry where our enemies had sworn to destroy us. We would reaffirm that Jews still remained alive. We would begin a new life together, bringing forth a new Jewish generation, from that very spot.

We were married on April 29, 1949. Under the canopy I asked the rabbi to recite the *El moleh rachamim* (memorial prayer) for my mother, for my father, and for all the members of our families who had perished in the crematoria. As he began to chant the prayer, tears welled up in my eyes, and I began to weep uncontrollably. I could feel the presence of the souls of tens of thousands of those who had been murdered. Everyone present wept, and it was some time before the ceremony could be concluded. Esther and I embraced, and the flame that had burned so low for the Jewish people, once again flared high. I was 23 years old when the Nazis invaded Poland, and now ten years later, my youth had been obliterated. I felt like an old man at 33, but I was alive and I had survived the worst hell people had known. Now, it was time for a new life.

After we toasted *l'chaim*, we ate, danced, and sang *Am Yisroel chai* (The people of Israel live!). Everyone rejoiced in this former place of death, near the barbed wire enclosures where people had been stripped of their dignity and then their lives. Hitler had lost, and we celebrated to show we had survived to rejoice.

We returned to Munich, and two weeks later, we applied as a married couple for emigration to the United States at the American consulate. We were asked many questions: Where were we born? Where were we during the war? Had we aided the Germans? Were we members of the Communist Party? We answered all the questions and signed our names. They told us they would let us know.

We eagerly awaited a reply for eighteen months, during which time we lived relatively comfortably in Munich. Because we got along fairly well, I thought of remaining in Germany indefinitely. Esther, however, became pregnant in the late summer of 1950. She was determined that, if at all possible, her child would not be born on German soil.

Finally, we received a letter advising us to be at the consulate with all our belongings on December 15, 1950. We were ecstatic. We packed what we could and presented ourselves on the appointed day. Some military personnel loaded us onto trucks and took us to the port of Bremen. There, we lived in barracks for the next two weeks.

Early on the morning of January 4, 1951, we boarded an old American military transport ship, the *General Sturgis*. The journey began immediately, and on our second day at sea we encountered a terrific storm. We became seasick and unable to keep down any food. Poor Esther, in a bobbing transport ship, five months pregnant! The days dragged on endlessly. For eleven days all we saw were sky and water, and we were sick for most of that time.

Early on the morning of January 15, 1951, we awakened and I saw something I will never forget—the Statue of Liberty holding her giant torch above New York Harbor. We cried, cheered, laughed, and celebrated all at one time. The United States! Freedom! We had waited so long for a chance to live in freedom, and the day had finally come. As we disembarked later that day, I bent down and kissed the ground.

People from the Jewish Relief Agency met us at the dock and whisked us to temporary quarters. Later we boarded a plane to Chicago and then a train for our new community. The relief agency sponsored Holocaust survivors and refugees. Communities all over the United States donated money and time to help Jewish families resettle in cities around the nation. I had never heard of my new hometown and we knew no one there. But I worked variously at construction, as a bartender, and as a shipping clerk, learning to speak English and about American ways.

Menucha and Morris emigrated to the same town in Illinois a short time later, where they owned and operated a convenience grocery store for many years, raising two sons. One is now an attorney and the second is an insurance agent. Moshe also emigrated and lived with Menucha and Morris for many years. Yitzchak and Paula emigrated to Canada, Yerachmiel and Itke to the East Coast of the United States.

When I was able to, I became a United States citizen. I have lived in that same community since 1951, and I opened my own clothing store there in 1955. When I arrived in Illinois, I found that nearly all the elders of the Orthodox synagogue in town spoke Yiddish, having emigrated to the United States from Europe a generation before me. Once again, we read the Torah on *Shabos* and chanted the service without fear of being attacked by thugs, and we chatted in Yiddish before and after services. I always held closely to the religious training I had learned as a boy in Poland, and every year, on the anniversary of their deaths, I say kaddish for the people who died the day after Yom Kippur so far away so many years ago. I also say kaddish every June for Rachel.

Our first son was born just four months after Esther and I arrived in the United States, and two other sons were born soon after. All my sons graduated from medical school and are practicing doctors. We had established a new family in a new land.

Epilogue

Adolf Hitler died in a bunker in Berlin on April 30, 1945, just days before the end of the war in Europe. He placed a revolver to his head and fired, cheating the world of his trial. Many of the Nazi leaders were hung after Allied trials in Nuremberg, Germany, in 1947. Adolf Eichmann eluded pursuit for 15 years, until Israeli agents captured him in Argentina in 1960 and brought him to Israel for trial. After months of trial preparation and testimony, Eichmann was found guilty of war crimes and hung.

Nazi war criminals still remain at large today.

After emigrating to Canada, Yitzchak died in Toronto in January 1959. Paula moved with her children to Israel after Yitzchak's death.

Morris Abarbanel died on July 20, 1963, after he and Menucha had come to Illinois. Itke died in the United States on September 11, 1976, seventeen years after she and Yerachmiel had emigrated to America. Yerachmiel remarried and is living in the eastern United States.

Moshe died in Illinois on January 9, 1983. He never married. I often urged him to end his isolation, and he came close to being engaged a few times. But he always said that after Ethel Prawda's death, marriage did not seem right. My wife, Esther, died on July 5, 1984, and my sister, Menucha, passed away in the same city in Illinois a year later, on November 1, 1985.

* * *

Why have I waited so long to tell my story?

Soon after I arrived in the United States, a Jewish family invited us to have dinner with them. We gladly accepted, and we had an enjoyable dinner, until the wife asked me about Wegrow and the Jews there. By coincidence, she had been born and raised in Wegrow and had emigrated to Illinois many years before the war.

I began telling her. I was eager for everyone to know what had happened, for the world to know what had been done to the Jews. As I began to tell of the events of the Day after Yom Kippur 1942, she put her hands to her ears and yelled in Yiddish, "Stop! Stop! Don't tell me any more. I can't stand to hear this! Please, stop!"

I stopped. I was in a new country and didn't want to make trouble. She couldn't stand to hear. No one could.

Jews who had been born and raised in the United States told me they had done all they could. "We sent money. We prayed!"

"Money, prayers! We needed your help," I told one fellow congregant at the synagogue. "We had money. They went to the gas chambers with money in their pockets. We needed action. We needed you to stand up for us!"

He became angry and didn't talk to me anymore.

Newspapers and newsreels carried reports about the concentration camps just after the war. People shook their heads and world sympathy helped to create the State of Israel. But people did not want the details. They wanted to forget. So I talked about it only rarely, if people asked.

I never forgot, but whom could I tell?

A new generation brought renewed interest, and over the years, young people who were born after 1945 learned about the Holocaust. But horror and time put a different edge on what happened. The young people learned only a little and what they learned had no impact. Numbers: 6 million Jews. Concentration camps: places with barbed wire around them. Choking gas and ovens: causes of death.

Just words.

Less than 25,000 Jews are left in Poland, and an entire way of life has been destroyed there. But what did the Poles gain in their cooperation with the Germans? The Jews provided commercial traders, hard-working professionals, a steady lifestyle, and a diverse culture that enhanced Poland. This is lost to the Poles and other Europeans, and over the years, that loss will become apparent. The Jews died, but in the end, Poland and most of Europe have forfeited a great treasure.

I lived through it. The Holocaust was not just words. A thriving culture of people harbored hopes, dreams, and goals. Six million all over Europe died, one at a time, each life a precious light that was extinguished. One at a time. And we must never forget and never let it happen again.

Both Jew and gentile must snuff out anti-Semitism anywhere it emerges from its vile depths. Jews must educate the world and never allow ignorance to surround them again.

Will my great-great-great-grandchildren have to flee the United States 150 years from now, because the world has forgotten and hate has once again replaced understanding? I pray not, but history says otherwise. Jews have always fled persecution. I hope that history is wrong, and that the awful events in Poland and Europe in the 1940s is the final lesson.

To this end, I decided to write a book, recalling everything that happened. I wrote in my native Yiddish. A rabbi translated the manuscript into English and my wife typed the translation. Still, I am not a writer and the manuscript languished for many years, awaiting revision and rewriting. Finally, a Jewish writer, who is a college professor and a former newspaper reporter, agreed to rework these memoirs into book form. This took about six months. The whole process took eleven years. Now it is done. I have fulfilled my pledge to remind the world of what I saw.

I, Shraga Feivel Bielawski, was born in Poland. I lived with my family in the town of Wegrow. Every word I have written is true. It has been fifty years, but I will never forget. I am the last Jew from Wegrow.

About the Author and the Editor

SHRAGA FEIVEL BIELAWSKI, a retired businessman, lives in Illinois. He emigrated to the United States in 1951 after leaving his native Poland in 1945. He grew up in Wegrow, a small town in Eastern Poland. During World War II, a thriving Jewish community in Poland was wiped out by the Nazis. Bielawski is one of the only Jewish survivors from Wegrow, where he had owned and operated a lumberyard and clothing store before the war.

LOUIS W. LIEBOVICH is an assistant professor of journalism at the University of Illinois, where he currently teaches courses in communications history and in reporting and editing. During a nine-year period in the 1970s he was a reporter for three different newspapers, including the *Milwaukee Sentinel*. His first book, *The Press and the Origins of the Cold War, 1944–1947*, was published by Praeger in 1988.